FOLLOW MY LEADER

Dr Murray Webb-Peploe in India

Follow My Leader

A biography of Murray Webb-Peploe

KATHARINE MAKOWER

KINGSWAY PUBLICATIONS
EASTBOURNE

ISBN 0 86065 288 2

The following abbreviations have been used for versions
of Scripture quoted in this book:

AV = Authorized Version
        crown copyright

RSV = Revised Standard Version
        copyrighted 1946, 1952, © 1971, 1973 by the
        Division of Christian Education of the National
        Council of the Churches of Christ in the USA

Front cover photo: Angus I. Kinnear

Printed in Great Britain for
KINGSWAY PUBLICATIONS LTD
Lottbridge Drove, Eastbourne, E. Sussex BN23 6NT by
Richard Clay (The Chaucer Press) Ltd, Bungay, Suffolk.
Typeset by Nuprint Services Ltd, Harpenden, Herts.

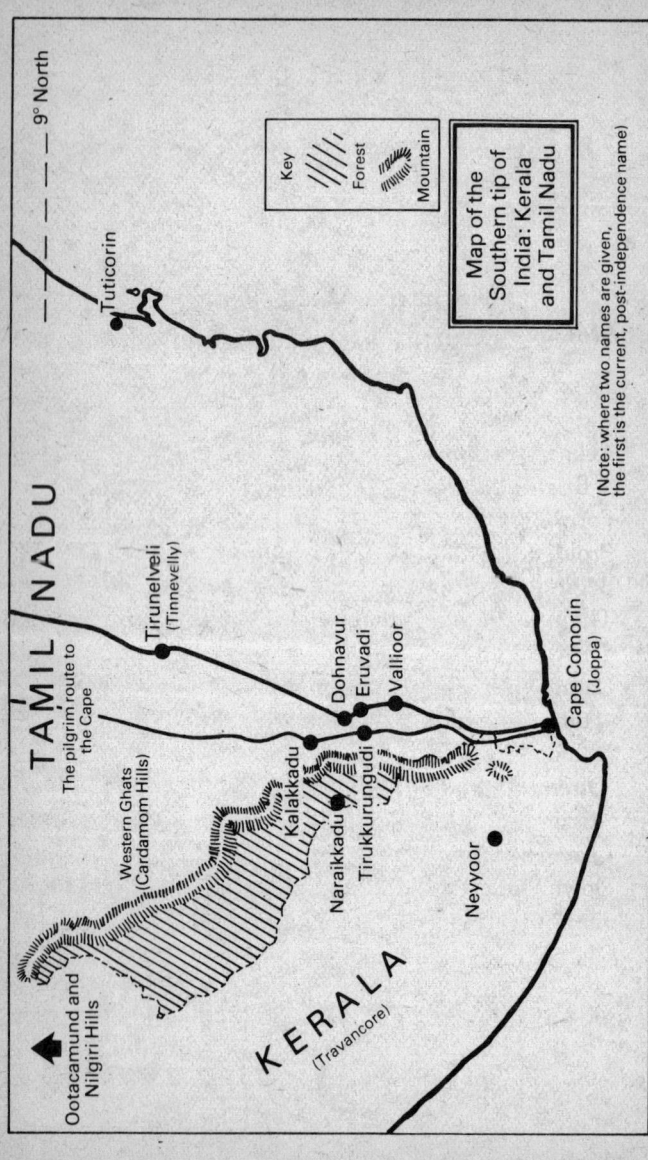

9° North

Tuticorin

TAMIL NADU

The pilgrim route to the Cape

Tirunelveli (Tinnevelly)

Western Ghats (Cardamom Hills)

Kalakkadu

Dohnavur
Eruvadi
Vallioor

Naraikkadu

Tirukkurungudi

Ootacamund and Nilgiri Hills

KERALA
(Travancore)

Neyyoor

Cape Comorin (Joppa)

Key
Forest
Mountain

Map of the Southern tip of India: Kerala and Tamil Nadu

(Note: where two names are given, the first is the current, post-independence name)

Contents

Acknowledgements

There are many people who have helped me with this book, and I want to thank them all: those who knew Murray and who have kindly given me interviews or sent me reminiscences in writing, and those who have read the typescript and given it careful thought. The Dohnavur Fellowship too gave me access to its archives as well as much kindness and encouragement.

Particular thanks must go to Murray's family: to Katharine for starting me on the project, and to Michael, Françoise, Hanmer and Lucile who have all contributed in important ways; also to my own family for their patience, interest and support; and finally to Dr Angus Kinnear of the Dohnavur Fellowship who has put in many hours of work and has entered into the whole thing with wonderful sympathy and enthusiasm.

Katharine Makower

A Brief Who's Who

This is to help familiarize the reader with some of the people in this biography.

Apart from Murray himself (1896–1982), the other main characters are:

Prebendary Hanmer Webb-Peploe (1837–1923). Murray's grandfather; vicar of St Paul's Church, Onslow Square (now Holy Trinity, Brompton) from 1876–1919.

The Reverend Robert Murray Webb-Peploe (1864–1904). Murray's father. He was first curate to his father at Onslow Square, then vicar of Christchurch, Millarville, Alberta, Canada. He died when Murray was nearly eight.

Evelyn Webb-Peploe (*née* Malan). Wife of Robert; mother of Murray and Godfrey. She brought up the boys on her own when Robert died, and went with them to China and India.

Godfrey Webb-Peploe (1901–49). Murray's brother.

Oda Webb-Peploe (*née* van Boetzelaer). Murray's wife.

Hanmer and Michael Webb-Peploe, born 1935. Murray and Oda's twin sons.

Captain Godfrey Buxton. Student friend of Murray's; son of Barclay Buxton. Founded Missionary Training Colony, Upper Norwood. Married Dorothea Reader Harris.

Dr Howard Somervell. Friend of Murray's; surgeon at London Missionary Society Hospital, Neyyoor, southern India. Took part in Everest attempts 1922 and 1924.

Dr Harold Ball. School friend of Murray's. His brother Alec, also a friend of Murray, was killed in action in the First World War. Murray joined his medical practice in the New Forest in 1947.

Frank Buchman. Founder of Oxford Group (later Moral Rearmament).

Dr Gordon Thompson. Superintendent, CIM Hospital, Hangchow, China.

'Amma', Miss Amy Wilson Carmichael. Founder and leader of Dohnavur Fellowship in southern India.

Foreword

I was with Murray in both preparatory school and under-graduate years, and have been in continual touch all the years since, and he seemed always to me a stretch ahead of most of us in mental ability and a foot taller than all of us in spiritual stature; so he has always been a 'special' to me both in love and respect.

It was a quality about him; and how it reaches the reader as we follow through the various stages of his life! From Gunner Captain in the First World War, after first confronting and settling for himself what he took to be the right attitude to war from his reading of the Scriptures; on into his powerful influence after the war in revitalizing the Christian Union (CICCU) at Cambridge, which continues so strongly today in its witness to Christ and the evangelical faith; then through his medical training and early hospital practice in London; and thus on to his China years, only leaving just before arrest by the communists. This was followed by his greatest twenty years with Amy Carmichael in Dohnavur, India; and finally the period with his family as a GP in the south of England, attracting such a number of patients that the practice had to be doubled.

There are those hundreds of readers, who knew and loved Murray, who will delight in all the details of these years; but I hope there will be many more who, having first read the early pages of his family background, will begin to find their hearts burn within them as they read of his daily walk with God, his seeking and findings of God's will, the abandonment in loving service as a doctor in China and India; and will then be caught up with the one and only consuming love of his life, not for bodily healings—though there were plenty of them— but wholly and totally the bringing of Christ to all those 'without God and having no hope'.

And this is the fascination of these pages. We learn of the special influences in his student days and onwards, which in a peculiar sense liberated him to be much more at ease in contacts with those not readily responding to the Christian message—influences that some criticized, but that were of special benefit to Murray and many others of us. This really prepared him for his life's work with that unusual almost irresistible attractiveness in his contact with others, with a naturalness, openness, humour, freedom, respect for others, which led straight on to ease in sharing the love of Christ; and it equally gave an originality and informality to his rich Bible insights and talks. The last chapter of the book, on his years in his medical practice in England, coupled with the wide-open hospitality in his family life with Oda and his sons, gives a heart-warming glimpse into the Spirit of the living God flowing into other lives.

The book also does not hide the strains, stress, times of self-questioning, even depression, the crises of finding God's will, in this man of unquenchable faith and endless love-action, well-called a 'troubadour of God' as in his own little poem:

> Make us glad troubadours of God,
> Loyal and guided, strong to dare,
> And free to ride the world light-shod,
> Living to love, and lift, and share.[1]

My special hope is that, in this book, which relates persistent service rather than dramatic incidents, readers will penetrate through to the riches that are communicated from spirit to spirit, as we continue to catch the beauty and glory that radiates from a life which could have risen to heights in the world, but which went the way of the cross and so magnified his loved Lord Jesus Christ by life and death; the life of one described by a colleague as 'one of the world's outstanding characters'.

NORMAN GRUBB

Prologue

One day, in the early 1970s, a group of hippies in brightly coloured kaftans boarded the London train at Southampton. Already in the train was an elderly doctor, a missionary to India in his younger days, who was travelling to London for a committee meeting. He had taken with him a modern version of the New Testament to read on the journey and, as he read, he began to pray for his fellow travellers. Almost at once, it seemed that God was speaking to him: 'I want you to give them that New Testament.'

We take up the story in the doctor's own words:

"Lord, they won't listen to an old square like me", I began. But then I realized that I must do it and asked, "How can I make contact with them, Lord?' I looked up, and one of them was lifting a fat bedding-roll on to the luggage rack. It was done up in striped calico, just how the Indians wrap theirs for travelling. So I took my book and went up to them and said, "Have you chaps been in India? Because your bedding-roll is exactly the sort we used out there and saw everywhere." They replied, "Oh, we've been in Morocco." So I sat down and asked, "Well what have you been doing there?"

"Just being."

"Is it a good life?"

"*Very* good."

I asked, "Why is it such a good life?" The chap sitting next to me was rather bleary-eyed—he was probably on drugs—and he answered me just one word: "Freedom". So I said, "Well that's all right; I suppose you mean freedom from a 9–5 office job—that sort of thing", and they nodded. So I said, "There's one sort of freedom I've found I simply could not achieve on my own, and that's freedom from myself. There's only one person in the world I know who can give you that sort of freedom." My bleary-eyed friend looked faintly interested: "Who's that?"

"The Lord Jesus Christ," I replied; and his next remark rather hurt—it was so patronizing. He said, "Oh Christ—he was OK." I said, "You're absolutely right—he was OK. And what's far more important, he *is* OK, because he's here in this carriage with us now."

They talked for the rest of the journey and at Waterloo they parted. The young people headed for Piccadilly Circus, taking with them the New Testament their new friend had given them, and Murray—for it was he—went on about his business.

Another scene, more recent still—Canada, 1982. An American family are on holiday; one of them describes a visit to the little country church of Sheep Creek, near Calgary, out in the foothills of the Rockies:

There it stood, nestled among the hills, serene and strong. The spruce logs of which it was built had been placed together in vertical fashion, drawing one's gaze irresistibly upward to magnificent sky and scudding clouds. Who had cared enough to build such a church in this wild and lonely place?

The door was open, inviting us to enter. Obviously the place was loved, even by the insects. A small termite-like creature had stripped the bark from the logs, leaving behind an interesting etching—almost as if by design. Narrow plain glass Gothic windows not only admitted light, but gave pleasant glimpses of the surrounding countryside.

What drew our attention most of all, however, was a picture of the founding pastor that hung inside. His name was Robert Murray Webb-Peploe! It was as if the curtain of time had suddenly been pulled back. And there he was, a quiet kindly young man, with a determination to make this lovely place, in the shadow of the majestic Rockies, something beautiful for his God.

Gently we lifted the picture from the wall and turned it over. There, underneath the data, was written the timeless message: "For God so loved the world, that he gave his only begotten Son, that whosoever believeth on him, should not perish, but have everlasting life."

Later, while in the neighbourhood, we had the joy of a reunion with Miss Cathy Nicoll—staff member of the Inter-Varsity Christian Fellowship. She had been my high school leader in Toronto and is now almost a legend in her time. She too had been startled by the picture on the wall at Sheep Creek. "It was Godfrey Webb-Peploe, you know", she said, "who changed my life. I met him years ago, in China."

We knew, of course, that Dr Murray and his brother Godfrey had worked as missionaries in Dohnavur, south India. There Godfrey had directed the boys' work while Murray had served in the hospital—spiritual giants, both of them. Was Robert, then, their father? It seemed unlikely. The dates looked somewhat early—and he had died so young. Then, too, the boys had been raised in England.

So we wrote to Dohnavur, and learned that Dr Murray, now a very old man, was living in England. Inquiry would be made. But before word came, God had called him to his heavenly home. Godfrey had preceded him, by many years. Now, it seemed, we would *never* know! [The writer is Mrs Edna Schwarz, Hon. Sec. to the Dohnavur Fellowship in America.]

The writer finished her account, and posted it off to England. Why? She had no idea that a biography was being prepared; it was just one of God's mysterious ways.

One last recent episode concerns my own meeting with Murray Webb-Peploe. I had offered to help him collect his memories together for some sort of a book. Being eighty-five and almost blind, he could not do it unaided. One sunny day in November 1981 I drove down to Woodley, their large house in Lymington. He and his wife came out to meet me. He was genial, welcoming; she was one of the most beautiful old ladies I have ever seen, serenely smiling, silver-haired. He talked non-stop and fascinatingly for the remainder of the morning, and throughout lunch. We ate in their large airy kitchen with its old-fashioned range and huge dresser with blue china on the shelves. After lunch Murray, blind though he was, washed up, still talking, while I dried. At about four o'clock, after a cup of tea, he led us in prayer and then I left, planning to visit them again after Christmas. It was the winter of the heavy snow, and in January Murray telephoned, with typical thoughtfulness and courtesy, to suggest that I should postpone my visit until the roads were better. By the time the proposed date came, he had gone, quite suddenly, to heaven, and the job of writing this book was left to me. Digging through his papers, I found a remarkable man, one through whom many lives were changed. 'Murray and Godfrey—spiritual giants, both of them'; what can we learn about the lives of these two men?

1 Beginnings:
The Wild West, 1896–1904

On August 24th 1899 a young mother sat in her hotel room overlooking the glorious Bow River Valley and the Rocky Mountains at the Banff Springs Hotel in Banff, Alberta, Canada, and wrote this letter to her little boy, Murray, who was then nearly three:

> My own darling little Murray,
> In case Daddy and Mummy should be killed on the railway and never come back to their darling little son, they want you to know that they long more than anything else that you should grow up to love and follow the Lord Jesus and to seek to glorify him by your life, and to seek to lead others to know him.
> Your very loving mother and father, E.M.G.W-P and R.M.W-P

They knew no child psychology in those days, but they were familiar with death. Whether the letter was actually sent, or just put by in case of accident, we do not know. At any rate, Murray's parents were not killed on the railway; they returned safely to the log-cabin vicarage and wooden church at Sheep Creek where Murray's father, Robert Murray Webb-Peploe, was vicar. Little did they know how their hopes for their son would one day be fulfilled.

Robert and his wife Evelyn had come to Canada from England some six years previously, after marrying at St Paul's Church, Onslow Square, London, where Robert's father, the well-known evangelical preacher Prebendary

Hanmer Webb-Peploe, had already been vicar for sixteen fruitful years and continued for another twenty-four. Born in 1837—the year that Queen Victoria came to the throne—Prebendary Hanmer Webb-Peploe was an outstanding spiritual leader. As an undergraduate at Cambridge he had made his mark in another way—he had been one of the very few ever to have leapt up the steps from Trinity Great Court to the Dining Hall from the bottom to the top! It was while at Cambridge that he went to watch the Derby, and was given, to his annoyance, a tract. The following winter he found it was still in his coat pocket, so he decided to read it. It was through this tract that he came to faith in Christ.

Hanmer was extremely athletic and represented Cambridge successfully against Oxford in both jumping and swimming. However, his sporting activities led to a severe accident: he fell from a cross-bar in the gymnasium and had to spend many months on his back. While immobilized he learned a great deal of the Bible by heart, including the whole of the epistle to the Romans, and still managed to get his degree. On leaving Cambridge, he was ordained.

After some years in a parish near his family home (where he was long remembered as the parson who jumped the five-barred gates instead of opening them!) he was on holiday by the sea with his wife and children, Robert among them. They were poor and, in spite of real faith and trust in Christ, he often felt weary and defeated. He longed to experience God's rest in all circumstances, but did not know how this could be found. Something happened there, though, that changed his whole life:

> While we were there my little child that was with us at the sea-shore was taken sick and died. I had to carry the small coffin in my arms all the way home, where I buried my little one with my own hands. I returned from the burial and said to myself, "You have come home unexpectedly and in trouble and now you must speak to your people instead of letting your curate speak; you had better tell them about God and his love." I looked to see what lesson was assigned for that Sunday, and found it was the twelfth chapter of 2 Corinthians. I read the ninth verse, "My grace is sufficient for thee", and thought, "There is the verse to speak on". I sat down to prepare my notes, but soon found myself

murmuring against God for all that he called upon me to bear. I flung down my pen, threw myself upon my knees, and said to God, "It is not sufficient, it is not sufficient! Lord, let thy grace be sufficient. O Lord, do!"

An illuminated text hung over my desk. As I opened my eyes I was saying, "O God, let thy grace be sufficient for me", and then on the wall I saw, "My grace *is* sufficient for thee." The word "is" was picked out in bright green, the rest was in black. I heard a voice that seemed to say to me, "You fool, how *dare* you ask God to make what is! Get up and take, and you will find it true. When God says 'is', it is for you to believe him, and you will find it true at every moment."

That "is" turned my life; from that moment I could say, "O God, whatever thou dost say in thy word I believe, and please God, I will step out upon it." The very farmers began to say, "Mr Peploe does not seem as fidgety as he used to be." Two sermons a week were killing me then; now fifteen a week can be preached when God wills.[1]

It was almost immediately after this that Hanmer Webb-Peploe's ministry took fire. He became vicar of St Paul's Church, Onslow Square, in 1876, where he ministered to a large and wealthy congregation and sometimes had as many as 1,600 people at a service. The well-to-do sat below in their proprietary pews; other worshippers were distributed over the church by female pew-openers clad in long black dresses and white caps; the servants sat in the galleries under the watchful eye of Mrs Webb-Peploe. The vicar stood before them in his black Geneva gown, a tall, impressive figure with a great domed forehead, deep-set eyes and distinctive white side-whiskers. He spoke loudly and very fast when he preached, combining a quick wit and lively style with great depth and range of Bible exposition. In the course of his sermons he quoted from memory large portions of Scripture complete with chapter and verse, a habit that tended to make his sermons exceedingly long. He was later made a prebendary of St Paul's Cathedral where he was a popular preacher; he also became well known as a convention speaker, particularly at the Keswick Convention which was founded in 1875, and also in America. In November 1903 he was to lead a powerful mission to students at Cambridge University.

Hanmer's son Robert was also athletic, and was tall,

broad-shouldered and handsome, with fair curly hair. When he and Evelyn became engaged, their families were already acquainted through the church. Robert, like his great friend Barclay Buxton, was curate to his father at Onslow Square. Evelyn was a teacher in the Sunday school. She was Evelyn Malan, a descendant of a Huguenot family that had suffered repeated persecutions for its Protestant faith.

The engagement between Robert and Evelyn took everyone by surprise, but it was warmly welcomed. His mother wrote:

> My dearest Robert,
>
>   Your telegram has just come, and I do congratulate you with all my heart. I can't make out how you have settled it all so quickly. However has Evelyn seen enough of you to be willing for this! How strange to think that she will be our daughter-in-law. I hope she likes that side of it... I do want to hear what Mrs Malan said to the boldness of "only a poor curate". I am sure God's blessing will be upon this arrangement, because of the entire unity of hopes and aims—but *means* are a very necessary factor in married life....

Robert and Evelyn were engaged for two years, during which time Robert continued his curacy at his father's church. Sometimes, when Evelyn was away, he wrote to her —warm, loving letters longing for the day when he would 'have her to himself, and when *as one* they would seek the Lord's face together', reminding her that 'a woman's strength lies in her weakness and that the more womanly and tender she is, the greater help and comfort she will be to him'. He urged her to make him into the husband she desired, who shall best glorify God: 'Mind you do it now, and don't give up, or be discouraged if you find it a harder job than you at first thought. I am a rough and tough one, but I feel, darling, that love—steady, persevering, holy love— will be the power with which you will "manage" me and help me on in the ways of the right and noble for God.' He plans too that when they are married they will be 'very particular as regards Bible reading and prayer. I am confident that then we shall become by his grace "flames of fire in the service of our God".' A week before the wedding Robert wrote to Evelyn, saying he was looking forward to the time 'when you get back into my arms'. His father wrote too, hoping that Evelyn would find the wedding perfect 'in things bodily *and* spiritual'. He added, 'Don't be afraid or ashamed to enjoy yourself! (1 Tim 6:17—end). God means us to be happy (as well as joyful) when we can.'

Sadly, at about this time, it was found that Robert had the beginnings of pulmonary tuberculosis and was advised to leave England. And so they were married and set out for Canada. But after a year and a half of marriage, Robert was seriously ill. Fron Denver, Colorado, Robert wrote home of the inflammation in the lung that had laid him low. He added, 'Evelyn is such a dear sweet wife to me—so loving and patient…she could not have done more for me during my illness than she has done. I tell her my one sadness is that I am such a wretchedly weak and infirm husband for her.'

Robert recovered, and soon they were established in Canada's Wild West where Robert had been given the post of pastor to the big ranching parish of Christ Church at Sheep Creek, in the foothills of the Rocky Mountains, 30 miles west of Calgary. Here the ranchers built under his direction a little log cabin that was to be their home, and a simple log church. The design of these buildings was unique. It was Robert's idea to build them of spruce logs placed in an upright position, and when the local residents worried that such a building would not withstand strong winds, the contractor agreed to receive no payment for his work until the building had been standing for three months. It is still there, eighty years later! Here Robert began his ministry in which he combined vigorous biblical teaching and preaching with practical care for the pioneering settlers in his parish.

At Calgary, on September 5th 1896, their first son, Murray, was born. His early childhood was wonderfully happy and free. His mother was often occupied with household tasks and parish concerns so the little boy was soon able to spend more and more time in the open air. Once a year he would watch the round-ups when the cowboys collected together the cattle for branding. They built a corral and Murray would be held up on top of the rails to watch them throw the cattle and brand them. Evelyn was helped in the house by a succession of feckless Irish girls who broke nearly all the crockery. They used to frighten Murray by telling him that the coyotes—the prairie wolves that hunt in packs—would come and eat him up. This image haunted him, such that he wouldn't go to bed without a light until he was thirteen.

The winters were extremely cold—minus 30 or 40 degrees centigrade. The milk in winter did not come in bottles but in square frozen blocks—you bought it by the frozen pound. It was a tough life, but the ranchers and their families were the little boy's friends. Sometimes he went with them into the local saloon and gazed at the slogan above the piano: 'Don't shoot the pianist—he's doing his best!'—a slogan that he carried into other fields in later life.

Discipline was firm. On one of his birthdays Murray was given a pen-knife and, inevitably, his initials appeared on a piece of furniture in the house. He was sent outside to cut himself a switch, and in the process cut his finger; the switch was duly applied to his rear and he was sent supperless to bed. Here the bread poultice came in useful, as the only thing he had to eat.

On another occasion Murray was rude to a guest. His father chased after him to beat him but Murray escaped by climbing up into a haystack and hiding there all day. Poor Robert was not well enough to follow his energetic young son up a ladder, let alone a haystack. But as darkness fell Murray surrendered—he was very hungry and he feared the coyotes would be roaming.

Murray became a believer in the importance of firm, loving disciplining of children for the rest of his life, for there was much love behind the discipline. The little boy felt secure; a security pictured perhaps in his memory of standing safe-held between his father's knees, as Robert sat with a copy of the *Illustrated London News* and showed Murray the pictures of the Boer War.

Robert and Evelyn's second child, Godfrey, was born in 1901 while they were still in Canada, but because Robert's health was deteriorating it was decided in 1902 that he must give up his work and return home to England. A few of the settlers gathered at the vicarage in April and presented him with a purse of 300 dollars which was subscribed by people of every denomination in and around Sheep Creek. Mr M. T.

Millar, after whose family the area had become known as Millarville, read an address in which he asked Robert to accept the purse 'as a slight acknowledgement of your sterling worth and the work accomplished by you in this district, both as a clergyman and as a man. We have always received the greatest kindness and help at all times from yourself and Mrs Webb-Peploe.' Robert was touched; he had grown to love his parishioners on the prairie. He hoped one day to return.

When the little family arrived in England, Evelyn took the two boys to her parents' home while Robert went to the Cotswold Sanatorium, near Stroud, in a last attempt to reverse the rapid decline in his health. The Malans' home was at 42 Stanhope Gardens, South Kensington, and six-year-old Murray found life there very tedious and restricted after his happy freedom at Sheep Creek. Evelyn's father had married a second time after her mother's early death, and his second wife was, to use Murray's own words much later, 'rather a snorter—she wasn't awfully nice'. The London parks compared poorly with the raspberry-strewn foothills of the Rockies. One day, when the boys were being taken for a staid walk in Hyde Park, Murray ran away and for a while got lost; but the free life of the prairies was not to be regained that way.

Meanwhile, Robert was struggling against his illness in the Cotswolds. He wrote lovingly to Murray sending him a blue feather he had found in the woods, and commented on the fine time he was sure Murray was having in London! He wished he were well enough 'to take dear Mummy and you about to see all the fine things', reminds Murray to take great care of his mother and Godfrey for him, and talks of coming home at the end of July. He also wrote hopefully to Evelyn of how he was gaining weight and of how the doctor had told him he had lost that 'interesting' look of the invalid. He wrote about the possibility of a visit from her: 'I am rejoicing at the thought of seeing my own loving darling again and giving her a good big hug. She is all the world to me, and she has given me the two dearest little darlings we could have had. Kiss them from Daddy. I shall love to see Godfrey's sweet little ways when I get home.' And again, 'So little Babbin's mail-cart has come to grief—it never was very strong. You must certainly get him another—not collapsible this time.'

In spite of his temporary improvement, though, the disease could not be checked for long. He left the sanatorium and the family moved to Fleet near Farnborough where they lived happily, Robert cherishing each precious moment with Evelyn and proudly watching his boys grow and develop. But he was growing weaker all the time, and on Sunday, August 14th 1904, shortly before Murray's eighth birthday, he went peacefully to be with his Lord.

2 The Fatherless and the Widow, 1905–15

After Robert's death, Evelyn and the boys moved to a comfortable house in Farnborough Park, not far from Fleet. It was called Bracken Glen and, apart from spells when they let it, it was to be their home for many years. Here, in June 1905, almost a year after her husband's death, Evelyn again sat down and wrote a letter to her sons. Like the previous one, written to Murray at Sheep Creek, this letter seems curiously prophetic, although the separation that she feared did not take place:

> My dearest little lads,
> I am writing this letter in case I should be taken away from you—up to heaven—to say that your dear Daddy when he was leaving us said to me, 'Live for the boys—they both have very different characters, but the Lord will make use of them in the world for his glory.' Your mother's prayer for you both is that God will make each of you 'a man after his own heart'.

It seems, looking back, as though God had given the dying father a special insight into his boys' future as he watched and prayed for them, knowing he must leave them so soon.

Evelyn at once took up the task her husband had laid upon her. Having settled into their new home, the next duty was to find a suitable school for Murray. Evelyn and Robert seem to have talked this question over before he died and the plan was that Murray should go to Eagle House, at Sandhurst. It was one of the oldest English prep schools, and had the great advantage that its headmaster was the Reverend Dr A. N. Malan, Evelyn's uncle, an interesting man of many talents. Most of the stained glass windows in the school chapel were designed and painted by him and , besides being the author of several school stories, he wrote hymns—one of which had been sung at Robert and Evelyn's wedding.

Murray started his new life with enthusiasm in January 1905. He enjoyed his lessons and did well at them. He also loved sport, and is mentioned in the school magazine as having made an impressive number of catches—twenty-one, far more than any other boy. Unfortunately, the atmosphere in the school was not an entirely happy one. There was much swearing among the boys, and the bullying was brutal: small boys would be tied to chairs and placed so near to the fire that they were almost roasted; or made to run the gauntlet of tennis balls hurled at their heads. Dr Malan, admirable man though he was in many ways, seemed unconcerned about— or possibly unaware of—what was going on. Although friendly and well able to stand up for himself, Murray wasn't completely happy here. Often his thoughts went back to the prairies and the good days when his father was alive.

Whether because of the rough atmosphere of the school, or because of Dr Malan's retirement that took place then, Murray left the school after a year and went to South Lodge in Lowestoft, Suffolk. Life was happier here, and Murray made good friends, in particular with Norman Grubb (whom Murray was to meet again at Cambridge) who remembers:

It was a good boys' school of about fifty boys. The headmaster was a clergyman—the Reverend Richmond Phillips. He made us learn passages of Scripture by heart, and we always completed the term by standing in a full circle in the gym and repeating the special chapter we had learnt. I always prided myself on getting that correct and therefore doubtless Murray did, who was top over me. I well remember doing Romans chapter 8 one term, and 1 Corinthians chapter 15 another. My chief recollection of Murray is of our fierce competition to come out head of the school. It was a close race, but Murray won, and that put me in my place for he was exactly a year younger than I.

This early training meant that Murray, like his grandfather, was always able to quote Bible passages with chapter and verse from memory. As well as hard work, though, there was plenty of fun—secret feasts at midnight and fishing from Lowestoft pier. Murray was also becoming outstanding at cricket. The school magazine records his once scoring forty-four runs in a school match and on another occasion bowling six wickets for five runs.

On the journeys between Farnborough and Lowestoft, Murray passed through London and stayed with his other grandparents at 25 Onslow Gardens. Things here in the vicarage were formal and regulated. After lunch, on the dot of 3 p.m. every day, Grandfather's top hat was taken out of the cupboard and he and Mrs Webb-Peploe would go visiting in the parish.

Sundays there were hard work: church twice in the day, with Grandfather's forty-minute sermons. Once Murray, seated with his grandmother behind rows of demure girls from a nearby boarding school, observed the long hair of two of them hanging over the back of the pew in front. The temptation was too much. While his grandmother's head was turned towards the preacher, he surreptitiously tied the two sets of tresses together. For a few moments nothing happened; Murray contemplated his work with satisfaction. But when the girls attempted to stand for the closing hymn chaos broke out and Murray was swept out of church to be later beaten—a beating that seemed to him a little hard as he had always understood that no work should be done on a Sunday.

When he was twelve, Murray won a scholarship to Weymouth college, and he started there when he was thirteen in September 1909. The South Lodge school magazine recorded that 'M. H. Webb-Peploe who entered for a classical scholarship at Weymouth College came out top of the list and his papers were so extremely good that the Council raised the value of his scholarship to £50 per annum, which is only done in the case of an exceptionally strong candidate. There is no doubt that had he remained here till next summer, as he will even then be well under 14, he would have captured one of the big scholarships at almost any public school.'

By this time the family had let Bracken Glen and had moved to Papillon House, Shorncliffe, Kent, where, partly to meet the bills, Evelyn had taken over the running of a soldiers' home. Here Murray met some fine Christians among those invited by his mother to give talks to the men. Evelyn did an excellent job at Shorncliffe; years later some of the men writing to Murray paid her tribute: 'We have many happy memories of the best of all stations but most of all do we revere the memory of your dear mother who was such a spiritual help to us all.'

For their summer holidays Evelyn took the boys to the seaside, always choosing to go to a place where a beach mission was being held by the Children's Special Service Mission (CSSM). She knew that here they would have lively company and good fun with games and activities organized by enthusiastic young men who in some small measure would provide the boys with what they lacked through not having a father. Most of all, she knew that from them they would hear the good news of Jesus proclaimed in a vital and attractive way. She longed more than anything that her sons would be drawn by Christ to place their lives unreservedly in his hands. Much to her happiness, it was on the beach at Swanage, in the summer before he started at Weymouth, that Murray turned to Christ and signed his name to the following: 'Being convinced that I am a sinner, and believing Jesus died for me, I now accept the Lord Jesus Christ as my Saviour and Lord.' He had known about Jesus all his life, but from now on he was to know him as his friend.

Weymouth College was founded in 1863 as an evangelical church public school. It was situated on the edge of the town, and its buildings were pleasantly laid out amidst playing fields, the open countryside and the sea. Murray arrived there as a scholar in 1909 and, as always, threw himself wholeheartedly into everything that was going on. He had a first-rate mind and an exceptionally retentive memory—an asset that never left him, even in very old age. He excelled in school work, particularly in classics and maths, and in anything that involved the use of words. He edited the school magazine for two years and was president of the debating society. The one thing he showed no gift for was music; he

loved to insist that he only knew when the national anthem
was being played because everyone stood up! He developed,
though, a love for poetry. Kipling was his favourite and he
often quoted him in later life, in particular 'Mulholland's
Contract'[1]—a poem about a man in charge of the lower deck
of a cattle-boat who, at a moment of great danger, 'made a
contract with God'.

> An' by the terms of the contract, as I have read the same,
> If he got me to port alive I would exalt his name,
> An' praise his holy majesty till further orders came.

Mulholland was spared, and the poem goes on:

> An' I spoke to the God of our contract, an' he says to my prayer:
> 'I never puts on my ministers no more than they can bear.
> So back you go to the cattle-boats an' preach my gospel there.
>
> For human life is chancy at any kind of trade,
> But most of all, as you well know, when the steers are mad afraid;
> So you go back to the cattle-boats an' preach 'em as I've said.'

Many seminal ideas of Murray's life are in fact to be found in
that poem: the personal relationship with God, the need for
obedience, the sense of being 'under orders'. It was while at
Weymouth too that Murray began writing poetry himself. At
this stage it was only at the schoolboy level, but it gradually
developed into a valuable and effective expression of his
feelings. Most people stop writing poetry once they leave
school, but Murray wrote poems throughout his life, and
more so in old age.

The other realm in which he continued to excel was sport.
He was in the 1st XI cricket team from 1911–14, won his 1st
XV colours for rugby, and was victor ludorum for aquatic
sports in 1914. Godfrey followed his brother to Weymouth
and, if anything, his career through the school was even more
meteoric. He too won every possible sporting distinction,
being twice captain of cricket and three times in the 1st rugby
XV, ending as rugby captain in 1919–20. Both brothers were
devastating fielders and it was reckoned that between them
they must have made over 100 catches in 1st XI fixtures.

Unlike Murray, Godfrey was very musical. He had too an innate love of wildlife, and bird-watching was one of his hobbies. Murray was head prefect; Godfrey was head of school. One contemporary remembers Murray by 'the high standard of decent wholesome Christianity which not only gained him the respect and regard of his contemporaries but left behind a tradition of decency and order'. Both he and Godfrey seem to have contrived to be good without being bores or prigs. They were very different in character. Murray was an extrovert and impetuous; Godfrey was quieter, more thoughtful. They differed too in looks: Godfrey was tall and lithe, with a long serious good-looking face reminiscent of his father; Murray was nearly as tall but more burly, and always with a good-natured cheerful smile.

It is remarkable that they always managed to be such fun. The high standards that were set for them might have crushed some. Thus in October 1913 Murray's grandfather, the Prebendary, conscious of the boys' lack of paternal guidance, wrote Murray a long and earnest letter urging him to resist 'the temptations that come to a schoolboy as he ripens on towards real manhood', in particular 'the bodily evil with its wicked passions and filthy actions'; and the temptations to the mind through 'evil literature that may be put before you. Let your power of study (which happens to be considerable) be given entirely to that which is noble and for the edification of those around you.'

Murray made many friends during his time at Weymouth, and made a point of keeping in touch with them in later years. He also formed good friendships on the CSSM beach missions at Swanage and other seaside places where he and his family spent their summer holidays. The mission teams included some medical students and it may have been through contact with these that, at about the age of sixteen, Murray began to feel that God was calling him to be a medical missionary.

In the summer of 1914, his last year at school, he went to help at a seaside mission on the Isle of Wight, and there he met two more medical students who were to become life-long friends. One was Howard Somervell who would later work as a surgeon in south India. Exceptionally gifted, he showed promise as musician, artist and mountaineer as well as in medicine. The other was Algie Stanley-Smith, then acting house surgeon at St George's Hospital, later to serve Christ in the remarkable revival in the Kigezi district of western Uganda. Algie asked Murray at the end of the beach mission to go back to St George's with him for a few weeks to help look after the wounded from Mons. Many medical students had gone off to the Front and the hospitals were desperately short of help, so Murray went. After this valuable experience he went back to school for one more term. He had decided to apply for a place at Cambridge; his headmaster advised him to sit the entrance examination in classics as he had not been taught science at school, and to change to medicine later. He was successful and was offered an exhibition to read classics at Trinity College.

By now, of course, the First World War had broken out. Many of Murray's contemporaries had volunteered at once; others had decided that they could not fight on conscientious grounds, and had joined the Friends' Ambulance Service instead. By December 1914 Murray was over eighteen and old enough to join up. However, he was still unable to decide between combatant and non-combatant service and so taught for two terms at Weymouth Junior School. Could it be right for a Christian believer to have a part, however remote, in killing another human being? He agonized over this question for over a year. In the summer of 1915 it became clear to him that as Christ himself in his dealings with military men never berated them for being soldiers, but dealt with the same issues with them as with everybody else, he should take a normal combatant role in the war, being determined to stand firm for Christ as he did so.

He decided, as many of his friends had done, to volunteer for the Royal Artillery, but to put in one term at Cambridge first—the autumn term of 1915. He recalled:

The change to medicine had not been very easy. I went up to Cambridge and had an interview with the Master of Trinity who was then Montagu Butler. He had been headmaster of Harrow and was a very definite Christian. He wrote the hymn, "Lift up your hearts; we lift them Lord to thee". I went to tea with him and he listened to my request. I was afraid he would say "no" as I had done no science, but he was extremely nice. He looked at me in silence for some time, and then he said, "My boy, you may read medicine, and perhaps you will be a better doctor for having read the classics." He also told me an interesting thing. He said, "Your grandfather used to come up and preach the university sermon quite often, and when he came he used to stay with me in the Master's Lodge at Trinity. One evening after supper in the summer, I took him out into Great Court. I said, 'would you come with me; I would like to fulfil one of the ambitions of my life.' So we both went together to the foot of the steps leading up to the Hall. I had always wanted to see together these steps and one of the three men who has jumped them from the bottom to the top."

'This jump', Murray went on to say, 'my grandfather had done as an undergraduate, although actually he was at Pembroke College. The second man to do so was Field Marshal Montgomery's father, who was Bishop of Tasmania in later life. The other of course was Whewell, a Master of Trinity—hence the name given to the jump, 'The Master's leap'.

So Murray completed one term at Trinity studying mainly biology and then, with about fifty other medical students from the university, he went into the Royal Artillery.

3 The Great War, 1916–18

December 1915 saw Murray starting on a gunnery course at Weymouth, together with a mixed bunch of men of differing ages and professions. Some were students like himself. One was a quiet schoolmaster, G. L. Mallory, who was later to take part in two post-war attempts on Everest. Murray was enlisted in the Royal Garrison Artillery, which during the war took over the heavier guns—mostly 6-inch howitzers and sixty-pounders. He was commissioned as a signals officer with the 62nd Heavy Brigade.

In mid-September he set sail for France with a draft of men, and late at night eventually found the sleeping quarters assigned to him, in a back street in Le Havre. It was only after he had settled down for the night that several discreet knocks on the door and the appearance of a girl in a night-gown revealed to him the true nature of the 'hotel' where he had been billeted. His main feeling was of pity for the girls, who were little more than children and had probably been tricked or forced into prostitution. However, there was nothing he could do about it and soon his attention was elsewhere: 'Although the flimsy bolt on the door was adequate to keep out those nightbirds, the bedbugs and fleas were quite another matter!' After this unpleasant night overseas, Murray tended to give billeting officers a wide berth and spent his nights where possible in a sleeping-bag in the open air.

The following day a perilous ride on a brand new motor-
bike over greasy roads took him to the Somme where, three
months earlier, on July 1st 1916, the famous allied offensive
had taken place. Of the British, 60,000 men had perished on
that day, 'a day of intense blue summer beauty, full of
roaring violence and confusion of death, agony and triumph,
from dawn till dark'.[1] It was here that Murray was to spend
the autumn of 1916 and the following winter, at the Artillery
Group headquarters.

He arrived on the night the tanks went up to the Front
Line. Spending the night in a shallow hole in the ground a
long way from any road, he was awakened by a strange noise
of powerful engines. The secret had been well kept, and few
knew about the new surprise weapon, the tank, as some
thirty-two of them rumbled up to attack for the first time at
dawn on September 15th. There were many problems with
the tanks: several of them, being new, broke down before
reaching the Front; many more were bogged down in the
mud, and nobody had foreseen what their caterpillar tracks
would do to the field telephone lines upon which all units
depended for communications. According to Murray, who
saw them arrive, British tanks reached the Front Line
cocooned in the telephone wires—with the loss of all com-
munication. Indeed Murray's first task as signals officer was
to try to get new field telephone lines connecting the batteries
with Artillery headquarters:

I found my Brigade headquarters in old trenches in Delville
Wood where I was to spend the winter as Brigade signals officer
to our four batteries: initially two of these were of six-inch howit-
zer guns, drawn by powerful four-wheel-drive lorries; the other
two batteries were of horse-drawn sixty-pounder guns. The horses
were lovely heavy-draught animals such as were used to draw the
brewery drays through the London streets. They had a terrible
time in the wagon lines. With mud over their fetlocks they were
often under enemy shell-fire. Their terror and panic were awful
to see, and it was a relief when the sixty-pounder guns were
replaced by more six-inch howitzers.

The gaunt branchless trees of Delville Wood were so full of
metal from the bullets and high explosives of the summer fighting
that it was impossible to saw them for firewood; no axe or saw

would survive. The trenches had been hurriedly constructed during the battle and there were human arms and legs protruding from the walls. They were water-logged, and you moved along on duckboards which were sometimes afloat. The officers' mess was just part of the trench with a gas-blanket separating it off at each end; the roof was made of galvanized iron sheets covered by a few sand-bags. We did not spend a comfortable winter but we made the best of it. Our mess-waiter had been butler to a well-known peer. He would draw aside the blanket that did duty for a door, and with a magnificent bow announce to the colonel, "Dinner is served, Sir"—dinner normally being bully beef and spuds, followed perhaps by ration biscuits (hard as boards) and plum-and-apple jam.

Brief extracts from Murray's letters written home from the Somme in 1916 show how he felt about his experiences at the time:

20th Sept: Here we are! A week in this joyful country.... The mud here is the limit and it poured with rain yesterday.

22nd Sept: V. interesting work up here, and quite worth doing.... We are living in sand-bagged dug-outs. I'm sharing with the Colonel for a day or two while we are pushed for room. Don't know what he thinks of my kneeling on a muddy French board praying! The Bosches are pitching a few shells some distance away on our right but they leave us severely alone, so you need not worry about my personal safety for it is, as always and everything, in the Lord's hands and that's the best place for you and me, mother dear!

5th Oct: It is good to be able to speak to the Lord when out in the rain and mud, but it is awful hard to get in a word for him. The sadness of this war is awful. I met a party of men struggling through the mud carrying stretchers, and just before we got up with them one of the wounded men had died. And to think that so many of those men die outside the gate of salvation in the Lord Jesus Christ.

Undated: It is Sunday again, just the same as the other six.... One has a great tendency in this life to slip into the habit of doing nothing—just sit around the stove and talk occasionally or simply do and say nothing.

3rd Dec: Found an Australian padre and six men holding a communion service in his "church"—a dug-out, pews were empty ammunition boxes; hassocks sand-bags. I do not think I have

ever enjoyed a communion service so much in my life. Kneeling
there you could hear the Bosch shells bursting in the distance
and just after the service was over the Hun put four over quite
near, two duds and two big explosions—just a Sunday morning
reminder that the war was still on!

24th Dec: We are very well off out here really but it would be
awfully nice to be home again and doing medicine…. We may
move soon.

They moved on in the spring, advancing through Bapaume.
On Easter morning 1917 the Front seemed quiet. Murray,
who had recently been appointed adjutant, had asked the
padre from Corps headquarters to come up and take a communion service for any who cared to join in. His brigade at
that time was covering an Australian infantry division on the
road between Bapaume and Arras. However, at dawn that
day the Germans attacked. Surprising the Australians who
were asleep, they broke through, over-running the field-
gunners. A message reached the regimental headquarters
that the heavy guns were being fired, quite unusually, flat
over open sights at the advancing infantry, and the Colonel
told Murray to give the order to continue firing as long as
possible and then to retire, removing the breech-blocks first
to render the guns useless should they be captured. Fortunately, Australian reinforcements arrived in a fleet of old
London double-decker buses just in time to drive the enemy
back, but the joy of the Easter morning had been stained and
spoilt.

Murray's letters continued:

2nd Mar: We are pretty busy and working nearly all day—
incessant telephoning and details to be fixed up.

20th Mar: Have been collecting dogs lately. Today we got a fine
mongrel, v. sporting and full of life. I took him for a long walk this
afternoon and he enjoyed himself thoroughly. His name is
"Jimmy"—and how long he will stay with us is another matter.
[In fact he stayed till the end of the war, when he was dressed up
in a small uniform, complete with tin hat and respirator, wounded
badge and staff gorget patches, and played his part by collecting
money for the R. A. Prisoners of War fund. What happened to
him after the war is not known, but his 'uniform' Murray kept
and took home.][2]

25th Mar: We had a great yarn, four of us, after lunch yesterday. The others were arguing against missions. They said they thought "religion" didn't teach you to play the game—so I said that was the chief thing that it did do among other things. We broke up though after I'd told them I hoped to be a missionary myself!

28th Mar: [to Godfrey]: You would love this country and its birds.

13th May: Another lovely day—and the country is wonderful, it being a case of "only man is vile". Have been having a read under a hedge here—it being Sunday. We are pretty busy at the moment; it is a great treat to be able to get away with the Lord and read, meditate and pray—three things which are needed a lot more. It seems to me that a lot of us Christians only go half way. We follow Jesus but we don't do it giving glory to God— leastways that is what seems to be wrong with me. The fact that I know Jesus doesn't seem to have affected the others to such an extent that they want to know him too. [This sense of failure was increased when one day Murray lost his temper and swore at a transport officer who had let the men down. The rebuke was deserved, but Murray was conscious only that he had failed his Lord.]

One day Murray heard that a battalion of the Dorsets was resting in a field nearby, on its way up the line and, as he had several old school friends in the regiment, he went across to see them. He found a school friend, Alec Ball, and they talked together in a ditch and read a psalm together. Soon the whistle blew for the Dorsets to move on. As they shook hands, Alec said, 'Anyhow, it is good to know that nothing can separate us from the love of Christ.' He was fatally wounded two days later.

Murray wrote about this to his mother: 'It is rotten—in some ways—about Alec, but he is now face to face with Christ in his glory. I had a letter from Harold' [Alec's brother] 'full of joy and peace. In those who know Christ it's not just despair or indifference—apathy—in those who are his it is peace and joy in spite of the sorrow.'

Soon after this Murray's brigade moved to Belgium, to cover the battle for the Wytschaete-Messines Ridge—one of the most successful battles of the war. On June 7th 1917 the Ridge was spectacularly blown up by mines and immediately overrun by allied infantry, but to Murray this attack, successful though it was, brought home to him the full horror of the war. He felt the situation acutely as 'groups of shattered and shell-shocked Germans stumbled back past us to captivity, still dazed and astonished to be alive'.

Again the brigade moved a little further north. Their batteries were located at the northern angle of the Ypres salient, behind the bank of the Yser canal, some 6 miles north of Messines. They were to cover the Passchendaele offensive—'a muddy bloody hell', as Murray described it. It had rained heavily; the ground was a morass. Their thirty-hundredweight guns were positioned on the ruins of Boesinghe Church whose rubble provided the only available solid platform for them. The infantry in the Front Line received punishing injuries. Although Murray didn't know it at the time, one of his closest friends at Cambridge, Godfrey Buxton, was severely wounded in this attack, and was to be lame for the rest of his life.

Murray's qualities of leadership were clearly appreciated at this time, as the following letters show. He also commented sadly on the death of another good friend:

4.8.17: The stunt which you have read about has kept us busy, and of course the rain has put the lid on things. The Colonel came in very bucked the other day and said he had been told by the General at headquarters that this Group gave them less trouble than any other. The Colonel was awfully nice; he said it was a great deal due to Rice and me and we must keep up the tradition! "Not unto us, O Lord, not unto us, but unto thy name be the glory."

7.8.17: Have just heard a very sad piece of news, that Jack Strain has been killed. He was out on this last stunt as observing officer and was killed in No Man's Land, where his body still lies. I believe they have not been able to get it in. It is hard for his people, though for him it is "long leave with pleasures for evermore at God's right hand". Somehow it seems that the best men get done every time. Jack was one of the best friends one could wish for. [He had become a close friend of Murray's at Cambridge in 1915; his sister later became the wife of Archbishop Coggan.]

After the Passchendaele offensive the brigade was given a few weeks' rest behind the lines. One day a squadron of the Royal Flying Corps rang up inviting them to bring over a side for a game of rugger, as it was too misty to fly. As the team, including Murray, arrived at the airfield the mist cleared and so the goal-posts had to come down. The Commanding Officer apologized: 'Sorry, chaps, there's a war on; we must fly.' But they invited the gunners to join them for a joy-ride. Murray described the trip, in a flimsy two-seater bi-plane:

> It looked a precarious kite; the fuselage looked like oiled paper. The observer's seat was behind the pilot's. Each had a kind of windscreen in front. There was no inter-com, only pad and paper. You wrote your message and pushed it over; the noise of the engine made speech impossible.
>
> The pilot headed east over Ypres, then over the German lines. It was most interesting flying over the salient. You could see the Front Line stretching away northward and southward. However, it was a gusty day and we soon ran into air-pockets and I began to feel air-sick and scared. I scribbled on my pad, "Are we all right?" The pilot looked round with a grin and wrote, "Sit tight and leave it to me." This experience has often come back to me as an illustration of living by faith in the Christian life. Just as I discovered on my joy-ride, so too in the Christian life, once air-borne, we must sit tight and leave it to God.

Murray later worked out a lively talk for schoolboys based on this experience. 'Faith: "Feeling Afraid I Trust Him".' We can imagine how they lapped up every word. Early in 1918, having been adjutant at the brigade headquarters for some months, Murray was transferred to 196 Siege Battery as second-in-command. This transfer to a much more dangerous position saved his life, as soon after his transfer a shell landed on the headquarters killing the man who had replaced him there. On another occasion, walking with a fellow officer along a railway line, a shell landed on the track between them. It was a dud.

After a short spell early in 1918 in the flooded area of Dixemude (when the flood water froze, the Germans sent over a raiding party on skates!), they moved south again in the spring to the neighbourhood of Arras, in France. The guns were in an orchard south of the main road, and the officers' mess was in a roofless bungalow with a tarpaulin stretched over the rafters. Here Murray had a favourite shell-hole in the garden where it was possible to be alone for a few minutes to read his *Daily Light,* a small India-paper collection of Bible verses that he carried with him throughout the war.[3]

One Sunday evening four officers were sitting at the mess table. Murray was writing to his mother; the other men were reading. Suddenly a game of *vingt-et-un* was proposed, and the Major turned to Murray: 'Peploe, you are no use, you don't play. Go down to the battery, take over and send the subaltern on duty to make up a four.' Murray obeyed, the exchange took place, and five minutes later a large shell landed and exploded behind the battery. Murray went back to find that there had been a direct hit on the mess: two subalterns were hurt, the Major was badly wounded, and the man who had taken Murray's place was lying on the floor with a gaping hole in his head. Thus for the third time Murray's life was spared. In each case he was deeply troubled, but resolved yet more firmly to yield his life fully to God. It seemed the only reasonable response.

The British Front Line south of Arras ran over a high chalk hill, Telegraph Hill, which had recently been captured from the Germans. On one occasion a German attack was expected, and it was Murray's turn to go up the night before to the forward observation post in the Front Line trench. The Germans were plastering the supply routes to prevent the British getting reinforcements up before the dawn attack next day. He described what happened:

> We took refuge from the heavy shelling in a flimsy dug-out at one side of the path on the back of the hill. We were there for an hour or two, and not surprisingly the talk turned to life after death. I discovered that there are no atheists in a Front Line trench. After a night with very little sleep, we stood-to long before dawn, but the assault never came.

Afterwards, Murray also associated that dawn on Telegraph Hill with the words 'My soul waiteth for the Lord more than

they that watch for the morning' (Ps 130:6, AV). He felt that
he had experienced to the full the stretched anticipation of
which the Psalmist wrote.

At about this time, Murray was awarded the Military
Cross. He commented on the award in a letter home dated
19th June 1918. 'Ever so many thanks for your letter and the
congrats. What the M.C. is for I cannot make out, or who did
the recommending. It may be just general work but it seems
all wrong that I should get anything, after having had such a
soft time compared with so many others.'

In September Murray was sent back to England, on a
three-week battery commanders' course on Salisbury Plain.
The weather was sunny and warm. He lived in a theological
college in the nearby Cathedral Close and drove out each
day to the gunnery range on the plain. He soaked in the peace
of the cathedral close in the September sunshine; it was
doubly precious after the noise and confusion of the Front.

All too soon he returned to take command of the battery, in
Belgium again. They were advancing towards Mons when,
on the night of November 10th/11th 1918, Murray received
orders from the Brigade commander to move the guns forward, and get them into action 'at all costs'. He queried those
words on the telephone as the enemy were retaliating vigorously as they retreated. The order was repeated; there was no
option but to obey. Murray described what happened:

> It was a beast of a night. The shelling was heavy. Some German
> battery had decided to loose off all their remaining gas-shells:
> 300—400 mustard-gas shells fell. The mud was awful; we had
> difficulty in moving our 30-wt guns, heaving on drag-ropes in
> gas-masks and total darkness. Some of us took our gas-masks off
> for short spells; we had more casualties from gas that night than
> for weeks previously. Mercifully none were serious, but all of us
> suffered from acute laryngitis and conjunctivitis, and could not
> speak or see properly for days. Even Jimmy, the battery pet, was
> puzzled when he attempted to bark but no sound came.

Although he had carefully obeyed orders over this offensive,
Murray was threatened with court-martial because of the
high gas casualties. Mercifully, the war ended and no more
was heard of the matter. It was on November 11th that

rumours came of a possible armistice and Murray and a
friend went into Mons. All night there had been heavy
fighting in the city: the Belgian civilians were killing German
stragglers. Murray went into the cathedral, where over a
thousand refugees were cooking, eating and sleeping.

He recalled: 'We walked to the main square and watched
the hastily organized victory parade: units of Canadians,
who were the first to enter the city, and of all other available
troops paraded jubilantly. It was indeed a memorable day,
and a privilege to finish the war where for the British army of
'Old Contemptibles' it had begun in August 1914.'

A few difficult months followed. The men, bored and
frustrated, longing to be demobilized, were hard to occupy.
Murray got various craftsmen in the battery to run courses in
their trade, but had to cope with opposition from some who
feared that if they shared their trade secrets, they might lose
work when they reached home. Games of all kinds were
organized, and football competitions held. Like Eric Liddell,
who refused to run on Sunday though an Olympic gold
medal was at stake but was prepared to break his rule to
umpire for imprisoned youngsters in a Japanese internment
camp, Murray 'played for the battery but rightly or wrongly
would not play myself on Sunday, though I organized the
games for any who wished to play—far better than spending
their time in the often bad pubs with the girls'.

Murray was always concerned for the welfare of his men,
and they liked and admired him. He also tried to maintain
Christian standards:

> I was the only Christian in our battery mess of six officers. I
> refused when second-in-command to run the drinks of the mess
> because I knew nothing about them. My teetotalism had been
> confirmed by the sad cases of drunkenness I had become involved
> with while in the army. Also, every time we moved, I managed to
> lose the rather lurid pictures from *La Vie Parisienne* which adorned
> the mess and to substitute rather nicer girls from the cover of the
> *Saturday Evening Post* which I collected for the purpose. The chaps
> finally put up with this and laughed at me.'

Not being an infantryman, Murray had been spared the
worst horrors of the war; nor did he allow what he saw and

experiencd to embitter him, as many did. He came home full
of gratitude to God for what he had seen of the bravery and
comradeship of ordinary men. He does not seem to have been
traumatized by his experiences as some were, who could
never speak of them. He often used them later in talks and
sermons to illustrate spiritual points, for the spiritual warfare
rather than the carnal was always the most absorbing thing
for him. The problem of pain and suffering was to be always
with him as he pursued his medical career but, as in the war,
he transmuted his feelings into action, while seeing the ulti-
mate resolution of the problem in the cross of Christ, where
the Son of God himself suffered on our behalf.

He was demobilized in February 1919 with priority as a
medical student. He referred once to the way in which God
had kept him, 'even through the war, although I was so cold'.
He felt himself to be far from God and useless to him; none
the less he recognized that three times he had been miraculously preserved, and this gave him a sense that God had
something special for him to do with the remainder of his life.

Almost at once on reaching home he became ill with the
severe flu that claimed millions of lives in Europe that year;
then he did a little teaching at Weymouth while waiting to go
up to Cambridge for the summer term. That Easter, Murray
and his brother Godfrey went with their mother for a holiday
in Cornwall. He recalled how one Sunday afternoon while
there he had an overwhelming feeling of depression. This,
looking back, seems hardly surprising. The experiences and
sights of the war alone would have been enough to plunge
anyone into a severe depression, as would the flu that he
caught on reaching home. Also, the change to humdrum
civilian life after the pace and responsibility of action at the
Front was depressing to many. But to Murray it seemed to be
none of these things. As he put it:

> I could not go back to Cambridge in the spiritual state in which I
> was then. I had let Christ down in various ways while in the army
> and did not feel fit to start my university career as a Christian. I
> read the Bible, starting at the beginning of Mark's Gospel, and
> soon found the passage where a leper came to Jesus saying, "'If
> you will, you can make me clean.' Moved with pity, Jesus touched
> the man, and said, 'I will; be clean'" [Mk 1:40–42].

Murray took this promise for himself. There was no immediate feeling of joy or peace; he simply took the promise by faith, believing that Jesus would cleanse him as he promised, just as he had cleansed the leper long ago.

So at the age of twenty-two, having been thrown from the cheerful warfare of the rugger field at Weymouth into the bloody reality of the First World War with an officer's responsibility for the lives of other men, Murray now felt himself cleansed and ready to continue a different sort of warfare for Christ at Cambridge, as in the spring of 1919 he went back to Trinity College to read medicine.

4   Cambridge, 1919–20

Murray was at Cambridge for only five terms in all: one before he went to the Front, and four after. This was because the normal university regulations did not apply to students who had served in the war. Although his time there was short, he used it to remarkable effect. And as Godfrey Buxton, his contemporary and friend there, has commented, 'That time immediately after the war was a pivotal period at the university.'

Leonard Woolf, a Trinity man of a considerably older generation, spoke of the fatalistic acquiescence in insecurity and barbarism that had gripped people's souls since the start of the war.[1] Vera Brittain who, like Murray, went up to university in 1919 having done war service—and having lost the people dearest to her—expressed the same feeling. She too felt condemned to live in a world without confidence or security, where anyone she held precious might at any moment be snatched away. She described how the year 1919 appeared as the spring of life after the winter of death, and she noted 'the reckless sense of combined release and anti-climax which sent her contemporaries...dancing in the vain hope of recapturing the lost youth that the war had stolen'.[2]

To some it seemed clear that things would never be the same again, and that the only way forward was to start from completely new assumptions. For others, including presumably Murray, the main feeling was that 'it was a good world into which the monstrous horror had broken, and we must build it up again, into something better, if possible, than we had before, but on the old principles and the old assumptions'.[3]

During the war the number of undergraduates in residence at Cambridge had fallen dramatically. For four years a 'deathly hush' had enshrouded the university.[4] Many colleges were used for military purposes, a situation neatly summed up in a contemporary cartoon. It depicted one officer cadet saying to another, as they watched two dons doddering across the First Court of Christ's College, 'Look at those two professors—wandering about as if they owned the place!'[5]

Throughout 1919 Cambridge was rapidly becoming normal again after its wartime depletion. When Murray went back there in April, there were two types of undergraduates at the university: those who had come up straight from school, and those who had served in the war. Differing attitudes were held by and about these two groups. Thus Vera Brittain observed the bombastic ex-officers on shortened courses determined to enjoy themselves (they had won the war, and they weren't going to allow anyone to forget it) and the boys just up from school who 'oscillated between a profound inferiority complex in the presence of the ex-officers, and a noisy determination to make their presence felt in this abnormal university'.[6]

The attitude of those younger undergraduates was expressed by Evelyn Waugh, also at Oxford, who wrote this to a friend in 1922: 'Oxford is not quite itself but the aged war-worn hero-type is beginning to go down. It ought to be all right again by the time you come up.'

There seem to be fewer accounts from Cambridge at this time than from Oxford, but Malcolm Muggeridge who went up to Cambridge straight from school in 1920 gave this interesting impression in his autobiography:

> There were a lot of ex-service undergraduates, men some years older than the rest of us, who wore British warms and scarves, and who had served in the war.... University ways and regulations understandably irritated them, and many of them seemed always

on the point of exploding.... In a way, they were tragic figures. At Selwyn a good number of them were ordinands, mostly in the Woodbine Willie [nickname for the Reverend Studdert Kennedy, popular frontline Church of England Army chaplain] or padre, style; a version of Christianity which emerged from the 1914—18 war, enormously sincere, ardent, and at the time seemingly vital, but which subsequently, for the most part, ran into the sand.[7]

This, then, was the Cambridge to which Murray came up for his second term in the spring of 1919. He was still tired and depressed after his war experience and the ensuing flu; and his first term was not completely happy. But his overriding feelings were of gratitude to God for his preservation and the determination to use his time to the full in serving him. He wrote:

> Up at Cambridge after the war, many of us medical students felt we had lost a lot of time. I still had the biology, chemistry and physics of the 1st M.B. to deal with, never having studied these subjects. I went to an experienced coach and said, "Do you think you can teach me enough in an eight-week term to pass the exam?"
> "Yes," he said, "I think so—if you are willing to work hard. I'll give you a list of the most likely questions—you can learn the answers by heart. You'll probably be asked at least 50% of these questions in the exam." I took the exam and passed. Then followed a year of anatomy and physiology with "bugs and drugs"—bacteriology and pharmacology—in the Long Vac term [extra term during the summer vacation] together with plenty of cricket.

In an early letter home to his mother, Murray wrote, 'Had a game of rugger on Tuesday and tennis today, so am getting plenty of exercise—in fact spending too much time on it if anything; must do more work soon, I think. We had a kind of test-paper on biology the other day and I did rather badly— only 37%, and in the exam you have to get 50% to pass.'

As well as studying hard and enjoying sport of various kinds, Murray was meeting up with several old friends and making many new ones. He said:

A new friend acquired that summer at Trinity was Carey Francis. He was a first-class mathematician and a very good tennis and soccer player. He just missed a blue for both these sports. In the Long Vac term, on a very hot night, we were talking together in the room I had temporarily in Whewell's Court. At the end we prayed together. He committed his life to Jesus Christ and said he was willing to go and do anything the Lord wanted. Later he became a maths lecturer at Cambridge and a don at Peterhouse College. While there, God called him to go as a missionary to Africa. He went under the Church Missionary Society as headmaster to a little country school in Kenya, and was later appointed headmaster to the Alliance High School, the leading public school for boys in East Africa. He did a magnificent job. He was strict on discipline and the boys loved him. Later, many of the leaders in the government and Civil Service were old boys of his school.

In fact Murray took every opportunity while up at Cambridge of sharing his faith with others. However, his efforts were not always well received. He told the following story of a time when God ultimately honoured his effort, although at the time he was rebuffed. One day he decided to call on a fellow-student called Sam Williams who had been a contemporary at Weymouth, although not a particular friend. Murray's enthusiasm made Sam's hackles rise, and after a while he cut the conversation short and, as Murray used to recall, 'showed me the door'. Murray felt sad that his witness had apparently failed, and left the matter there—or rather, with God. Years later, in India, he received a letter from Sam Williams who had inherited his father's farm in New Zealand and was now an active Christian. Sam told Murray:

One day, I was riding my horse along the range of hills overlooking the beach. I had just reached a steep point on the hillside, where there was a high wind blowing. As my horse turned slightly, the wind suddenly caught my cap and glasses and they shot out into the air over the steep bank. My immediate reaction was to swear. At once my consciousness was invaded by the presence of God. I was acutely conscious of indescribable love. There was only one thing for me to do and I couldn't do otherwise. So I knelt down on the grass and offered my life to God.

Apart from his medical studies and his sporting activities, Murray gave a considerable amount of his time while at Cambridge to the Cambridge Inter-Collegiate Christian Union (CICCU). Founded in 1877, this was (and still is) a group of evangelical[8] Christian students who met to encourage each other by Bible-study and prayer and who also looked outwards in the hope of leading unbelieving friends to faith in Christ. The CICCU, which had been flourishing in 1913–14, was extremely small by the end of the war. Not more than about fifteen students would meet for the daily prayer meeting among them Murray and his friend Godfrey Buxton. Another member was Norman Grubb, Murray's friend and rival at South Lodge School, also decorated and wounded in the war. He recalled, 'our surprise and delight when we met at Trinity, and immediately began to take our share in the CICCU DPMs [daily prayer meeting] at the Henry Martyn Hall. There were very few of us, but we were on fire for God, and we daily got down on our knees and poured ourselves out in prayer, particularly, of course, for the university. There was always life and we were a close knit group.'

Another contemporary later to become an African missionary, Joe Church, has described his feelings about Murray Webb-Peploe and Godfrey Buxton as follows:

> They were held in considerable awe. They were both captains in the army, and I was only a second lieutenant. Both had been decorated with the M.C.—Godfrey twice. Both bore names already revered in evangelical circles;[9] both had qualities of leadership. Godfrey was small and slight and had been so badly wounded at Passchendaele that he spent his time at Cambridge on crutches and was often quite incapacitated; Murray on the other hand was tall, burly, an outstanding sportsman. Murray was jovial, amusing, extrovert; Godfrey quieter, charming, courteous. They made an outstanding pair to lead the Christian Union out of the doldrums left by the war.

For this indeed is what happened. Norman Grubb has recalled how 'gradually our numbers increased to around fifty, with the Saturday evening Bible readings and the Sunday evening sermon'. This sermon owed its origin to Charles

Simeon, vicar of Holy Trinity Church from 1782–1836, who preached weekly to hundreds of undergraduates there. During the war these sermons ceased, but were restarted while Murray and his friends were on the CICCU committee; always they presented the Christian message in a vital and authoritative way. The minute book of the CICCU executive committee records that among those present on June 2nd in Mr B. G. Buxton's rooms at the first meeting of the newly elected committee for 1919–20 were the following: B. G. Buxton (Trinity) President, G. E. J. Foster (Queen's) Vice President, N. P. Grubb (Trinity) Secretary, and M. H. Webb-Peploe (Trinity) Treasurer. Later in the year Murray became Vice President, and for a short time President. Norman Grubb has recalled:

> Murray always seemed cut out for leadership, so it was natural for him to follow after Godfrey Buxton. We changed President more frequently than usual, because of the shortened war-service degrees. I myself left Cambridge early, to join my father-in-law, C. T. Studd, in the Congo. Murray and about twenty others came down for my wedding to Pauline, C. T.'s youngest daughter, just before we sailed for Africa, and I well remember the fun they put into the wedding, nearly damaging our get-away car!

By July 1919, a mission to the university was being planned for the following February. As Godfrey Buxton saw it, 'The war had taught us the importance of decisive action. In our year at Cambridge following the war we pursued this policy; we held a mission. There was a need both for teaching and for inspiration.'[10] So the CICCU grew, members at the daily prayer meeting increasing over the year from fifteen to about fifty. This was largely the result of the faithful and conscientious efforts of Murray and others like him who never flagged in seeking to win their friends for Christ. Thus Joe Church, who came up to Cambridge to some degree in rebellion against his Christian upbringing, was converted at a beach mission during a vacation and went back to Cambridge a very new Christian. He recalls how 'Murray and Godfrey Buxton "specialled" on me. They always took trouble to wave across the street, to talk and be friendly to me and to invite me to meetings.' By the time Joe Church left Cambridge he was rooted and grounded in his faith and was ready to be used by God in East Africa where, in Ruanda, a flame of faith was lit that has never been quenched since.

Godfrey Buxton has described Murray as he knew him at Cambridge as 'popular because he was cheerful and straight-forward. He was a good rugger player—that was in his character; he'd go hard for what he thought should be done, and could take kicks and rebuffs well. He was a good speaker at meetings and so on, but his genius was in getting alongside a fellow and leading him to Christ intelligently.'

Murray wasn't only concerned for the students, though; he taught in a local Sunday school, and took part in open-air meetings on 'Parker's Piece', an open space in the town. He wrote home one day, 'It was, I'm afraid, a bit of a struggle to give up cricket for the Sunday-school treat, but it was well worth it as we had a great time.' He also reported in a letter home a conversation he had had with his 'bedder' (the college domestic servant who made the undergraduates' beds and cleaned their rooms): 'Had a v. nice talk with my bedder, she is keen and lives it too. She lost her husband some years ago and her only boy died a prisoner in Germany. It is hard…have you a small book on comfort one might give her?'

Interesting light is thrown on Murray's efforts and influence in the personal recollections of Basil Atkinson, who went up to Cambridge in October 1914 and again, like Murray, in April 1919. He was later to become under-librarian at the university library and for years was one of the few senior members of the university to give support and encouragement to the CICCU. He once recalled 'I didn't at first join the CICCU, but in the Michaelmas term of 1919 my friend Murray Webb-Peploe persuaded me to join and I signed the form in his rooms at Trinity. So I owe my mem-bership of the CICCU to him.' On the other hand, Basil also recalled a time when Murray's enthusiasm had an inhibiting effect:

The Sunday morning prayer meeting was founded while Murray Webb-Peploe was President. He generally led it. It was very small and select and mostly confined to the executive committee members. Somehow I was allowed to go, but for a long time I was too shy to pray out loud because of the august status of the others there. My shyness was not helped but rather promoted by exhortations from Murray that they would like *everyone* to pray, which I thought were aimed at me. I have always looked back on them as just the way *not* to deal with shy people.[11]

While the CICCU was being revived with new life and energy after the depletion of the war years, it was also for the first time forming links with groups of Christians at other universities. Thus in December 1919 some sixty students from Oxford, Cambridge, London and Durham met in London for the first 'Inter-Varsity Conference'. Murray was chairman for the first day, and many things sprang from this conference—in particular the founding, in 1928, of the Inter-Varsity Fellowship (IVF; now UCCF—Universities and Colleges Christian Fellowship). Immediately after the conference in December 1919 a letter was published in *The Christian* as part of a correspondence following the publication of a book about Darwinism called *God and the Struggle for Existence*. This letter was signed by six university students, including Godfrey Buxton and Murray from Cambridge, and contained the following statement:

> The writers of this letter claim to represent those who do not accept as true either Higher Criticism or Evolution, where they conflict with the facts revealed by the Spirit of God in Genesis and the rest of the Bible.
>
> With reference to the statement that the vast majority of students accept the principles of Higher Criticism, we venture to say that a considerable and increasing number are finding that in accepting the whole of the Scriptures by faith as the word of God, they derive food and strength from every book, in daily life.
>
> We are witnessing term by term in the universities, through the preaching of Christ crucified and risen, such radical changes in the lives of men of various temperaments, abilities and types of thought, as are evidence that this gospel is still 'the power of God unto salvation' and that the blood of the Lord Jesus Christ is still the only remedy for the sin and evil in the human heart.

This letter was an important step in the voicing of a clear evangelical viewpoint at a time when liberal theology was gaining power and influence.

So at Cambridge Murray lived life to the full, and many lives were transformed through his friendship. He left university a year early, explaining:

> In the summer of 1920, three of us medics at Trinity lightheartedly decided to go in for the 2nd M.B. examination a year early—largely as a trial trip, to see what the exam was like. To our surprise we all passed, and so decided that as we were already three or four years behind our contemporaries because of the war, we should leave Cambridge and go on to medical school.

Thus Murray went on to St Thomas's Hospital, London, where he spent the next five years, but his links with Cambridge did not end. He became a member of the Cambridge University Missionary Band. This group was formed in 1922 for those willing to go abroad as missionaries and there were fifty-two members. Its formal inauguration took place at a breakfast held on June 8th 1922 at the Dorothy Café in Cambridge.

Murray's brother Godfrey, who was now up at St Catherine's College and President of the CICCU, is in the photograph taken on that occasion; Murray, fully engaged at St Thomas's, could not be there. Godfrey's time at Cambridge was used quite as much by God as Murray's had been. A full back in the Cambridge University rugby team, he gave up the opportunity of a blue in order to be President of the CICCU. He realized he could not manage both, as well as his academic work.

So in the four years since the war the CICCU had increased from fifteen members to one hundred, and among them were thirty-five, including the two Webb-Peploe brothers, who were later to serve Christ all over the world.

5 'Tommy's' in the 1920s: 'Buchmanism', 1920–25

The 1920s were in full swing. In London the young and wealthy, with Prince Edward at their centre, 'danced with feverish determination to shut out the memories of the terrible past'. The description is that of Frances Donaldson, in her biography of King Edward VIII. He was almost an exact contemporary of Murray's. She continued: 'Bereaved and uprooted and emotionally exhausted but with an entirely new freedom from convention, large sections of society spent their time in the pursuit of pleasure with a single-mindedness which marks this generation off from almost every other in history.'[1]

Murray reacted in a very different way. Bereaved, as they all were, but in no way uprooted, he pursued his course with energy and determination at London's St Thomas's Hospital —'Tommy's' to its students and staff in those days. 'In that autumn of 1920,' he said, 'Most of the clinical students were ex-service men; there were no women students except at the Royal Free. Many of us had a long record of active service overseas; some had commanded battalions or batteries. One had been awarded the Victoria Cross—a quiet, unassuming man.'

Several of Murray's friends who had survived the war were now studying and working in the London hospitals. One was Howard Somervell, who had served as a surgeon at the Somme. Murray gave us a glimpse of Howard, who was a

57

house surgeon at University College Hospital at this time:

> I remember walking down Tottenham Court Road with Howard
> Somervell, just after the first war. He was wondering what God
> wanted him to do with his life once his medical studies were
> completed. So, threading our way through the crowd, we both
> prayed aloud. You couldn't shut your eyes—that was fatal!
> Anyway God answered the prayer, and four years later Howard
> became clear that his life's work was to be at Neyyoor in India.

Soon after his arrival at St Thomas's, Murray was temporarily immobilized by the removal of a torn cartilage in the
knee—the result of a rugby injury. It was a blow, as he had
hoped to play a good deal of rugby. Later, though, he saw
God's loving purpose in the accident, for while he was a
patient in the hospital, his friend Godfrey Buxton asked an
American he had met in Cambridge, Frank Buchman, to
visit him there. This visit introduced Murray to someone
who was to have a considerable influence on him, and brought
him in right at the beginning of what appeared then to be one
of the most vigorous growing points of Christianity. It was
typical of Murray—eager, thorough, doing nothing by
halves—that he was soon in the thick of it: 'Buchmanism',
'The Oxford Group', 'Moral Rearmament', as it later became
known. It had no label at the time: it was simply a 'movement
of personal religion' started by Frank Buchman, a Lutheran
minister, with the aim of 'making the principles of the New
Testament a working force today'. The way in which the
movement operated was through personal friendship and
witness. In friendly personal talks men and women found
they could admit their moral failures and so become aware of
sin in their lives. They were helped to turn to Christ as the
one who could deal with their sin. Once converted they were
encouraged to continue by reading the Bible and by prayer.
In particular, Buchman emphasized the *listening* aspect of
prayer. This involved coming quietly to God at the beginning
of each day and listening for his direction which often came
in what were described as 'luminous thoughts'.

Godfrey Buxton, years later, remembered Frank Buchman
as he was then: 'Fr-a-ank Buchman was a great man';

Godfrey Buxton humorously drawled the name, presumably remembering how it sounded to him:

> He entirely lacked good looks and spoke with a slightly Germanic American accent derived from his Swiss immigrant parents. He had an amazing gift for personal work—for leading individuals to Christ. He certainly based what he said on the Bible, but he rarely spoke from it directly or spoke holding one—he said it might put off worldly people. I don't think, however, that he used the Bible as *realistically* as Murray and I had learnt to do. He tended to specialize too in converting the influential and rich—the 'up-and-outs' as he called them. He reckoned they were harder to reach than the down-and-outs, through having less sense of need. He had contacts everywhere.

Frank spent the whole afternoon talking with Murray of the way in which God can guide. As Murray observed, 'Personal guidance had been to me largely an unattainable ideal; with him it was a practical everyday reality.' He also described what happened next:

> Out of that visit arose a fascinating three months in the USA, for a few days later Frank asked Godfrey and me if we would go over to the States and spend the Lent term in the eastern universities —mainly Harvard, Yale and Princeton, sharing the good news of Jesus Christ and our experiences of God's presence with us in the war.
>
> "Ask God about it and he will show you," Frank said. The weeks that followed were to convince us of the three fundamental and practical facts concerning the leading of God: that God does guide; that where he guides, he also provides; and that he 'works at the other end', confirming and preparing the way. After praying about this invitation we both felt it right to accept, but the obstacles were many. To fulfil the programme we had to sail early in January 1921—that is, in three weeks' time. I was mobile again, but Godfrey's war wound was still sometimes breaking down and his doctors were doubtful about his going. I had to get a war-service grant interrupted, and to have permission from the hospital to miss a term, and we had at this short notice to get a passage across the Atlantic. When the other problems had been solved with less than a week to go before we should set out, I crossed the river to Cook's Travel Agency, and asked for a passage in the following week. The man behind the counter

looked at me, obviously thinking I was mad:

"Do you realize that there is a waiting list of months for America?"

"Anyhow, add our names to the list," I said.

"Oh, all right, but it is quite hopeless."

I went home for the weekend. On Sunday morning the first verse in my daily Bible reading was Matthew chapter 14, verse 22: "And straightway Jesus constrained his disciples to get into a ship, and to go before him unto the other side." It was cheering, but there was still that waiting list. On Monday morning, after the morning's ward-round and dressings, I went over to Cook's, and found my friend at the counter. He said, "You are the one who came in on Saturday, and I told you it was hopeless; but we have had an extraordinary number of cancellations for the Red Star Liner sailing from Poland to the USA in four days' time— let's look at the list." There were two berths: one first class, one second. I booked both, and when we were on board, the Purser told me there had been no more cancellations. Coincidence?

The second class was full of Poles emigrating to America. I watched one gentleman at breakfast dispose of a large fish by spearing it amidships on a fork, working down one side non-stop, then down the other, till there was only the skeleton left—still firmly and triumphantly impaled on the fork. The less said about that voyage, the better. It was terribly rough; the corridors and lounges were littered with uncontrollably sick Poles.

They reached New York several days late after the stormy crossing. Godfrey Buxton describes what happened next:

We were taken round all the great 'Ivy League' universities. A well-known American evangelist would be running a mission and our task was to pick up and retrieve any wounded birds behind the scenes—talking to students about Christ: how he had been with us on the battlefields of France and Belgium, and how he could be with them now. Frank Buchman took care of all the planning and finance; he knew all the rich old ladies! He was very keen on guidance. He would sit in a chair and "listen". Then he'd say, "God wants us to do this today." He was very strong on *listening*; almost before we did anything, we would listen to see if God had something to say about it.

Sometimes we just lived in a university for a while, talking to the students as we met them. We would be given a room in one of the fraternity houses, and people would come and see us there. At other times we stayed in fantastically wealthy homes. Some of these people would have imported an English butler, paying him a huge salary, just for the kudos. The butler would crease our trousers and lay out our pyjamas and do all the correct things—and we let him!

Murray was very acceptable to Americans. He had a loose, easy style and was always relaxed and approachable—much more so than I was. The students were responsive: we were officers and had been decorated in the war. They were intrigued with what we had to say, and amazed that it was Christian.

Murray in turn recalled:

We were privileged to spend a week in the Ivy Club at Princeton, and were welcomed with the warm hospitality then shown to all British ex-servicemen just after the war. In fact we were two of the few non-members of the Club ever to be invited to the annual reunion dinner in New York. We prayed over this invitation, not very keen to go, for in spite of prohibition the party was likely to be pretty "wet" with contraband, boot-legged or home-brewed drinks. Godfrey was not well enough, but we felt that I should attend. One of the students entertained me for the night in his parents' empty flat in New York.

There were seventy or eighty of us at the dinner and by 11 p.m. there appeared to be only four of us who were still sober. Chairs, decanters, glasses were being thrown around and finally there was a concerted move downstairs to migrate to a night club. I found myself helping a fifteen-stone university weight-putter downstairs and out to a taxi. That morning we had had a long talk about Christ, but he had protested, "I must get drunk tonight, and I can think about this tomorrow." I got him into a taxi with some difficulty, and then he began to be violently sick. Asked where his parents lived, his answers varied. I took the street number that occurred most often and fortunately we got it right and his door-key fitted. I got him upstairs in the lift, undressed him and put him to bed, and then ran into his mother who was greatly distressed. I comforted her as best I could.

The next day was most interesting: men were coming for talks all that morning. Charlie, the weight-putter, was in tears: "I know I'm breaking my mother's heart." He agreed when I said I had found that the sort of fun of last night didn't really make life more enjoyable. I told him that only Jesus Christ can really satisfy us, and I believe he turned his life over to him.

Interesting insight into Murray's feelings about this trip is given in a letter that he wrote from America to Godfrey Buxton's fiancée, Dorothea. It shows his humility and responsiveness to anything he felt would make him a more usable servant of Christ. He wrote:

I have learnt more in the last ten days than in all my life about this game, and it makes me feel how absolutely helpless and ignorant of it all one is. I may as well tell you how it seems to me. This work has convinced me more than ever of the amazing truth of the Bible, every part of it, and of one's belief in what it teaches, but I have been seeing, I think, that I have been allowing my Christian doctrines to be a barrier between me and the man who needs a Saviour and a surgeon. And I have not been getting down to where men live and sharing with them the mess I have been in and the temptations that come every day…. Also I am trying each morning in the Quiet Time to ask the Lord to show me anything that needs cleaning up and just jot it down and then get out and do it. It means sometimes writing a letter to someone apologizing for something I'd almost forgotten…. The joy and simplicity of life when one is really square with the Lord and with everyone round is just great. It all throws new light to me on 1 John 1:7—"If we walk in the light, as he is in the light, we have fellowship with one another, and the blood of Jesus his Son cleanses us from all sin."

By this sharing one gets cross-sections of men's lives, as "soul-surgery" puts it, in a way one never has before. Men seem to open right up and one can ask them plain questions, and they like it when they realize we are both just plain sinners. The hunger under the surface is very real; men come and talk of social conditions in England, Cambridge customs, etc., but once fling out a bait on these lines and they bite at once. If one can generalize, though it is always dangerous to do so, we in England who are evangelical are getting our air and food—prayer and the Bible—but are short on exercise; really getting where men live and diagnosing a man's trouble—'getting his history', as we say in medicine.

American houses are 'dreſful' hot and fuggy. We perspire and sometimes almost expire! And people *can* talk. I find my poor wee brain trotting along behind, so to speak, panting to keep up in the conversation. Sometimes one gives it up and suddenly finds one has said "Yes" where it ought to have been "No"—*et voilà*. But I have not told you half the comic things that have happened and the bricks we drop; it would need several three-ton lorries to carry them all. Anyway, life is just 'lots o' fun'.

In 1920 Buchman made Cambridge his base and, as Oliver Barclay commented:

> It tested the CICCU's discernment to the limit. Buchman constantly stated his faith in the whole Bible, the death of Christ and the second coming. He spoke of the blessing he had received at Keswick.... As time went on, however, disturbing features emerged.... The whole movement sounded more 'spiritual' than anything based on the Bible.... Many Christians felt they had to dissociate themselves entirely from their aggressive but biblically weak approach.[2]

At any rate, once back in England, although busy with his medical studies, Murray kept up his involvement with the 'Groups'. Indeed, with his infectious enthusiasm, he contributed considerably to their growth. An undated letter from a friend, Captain Loudon Hamilton, told how, 'I often recall and recount your coming over to Oxford in 1921 and I do bless God that he sent you and used you as he did with courage and real adventure in those days. The story of that weekend has gone all over the world, almost!' It was in Loudon's room that weekend that Buchman's work at Oxford had begun.

Frank Buchman was developing an attractive and effective method of reaching the less accessible 'up-and-outs': the house party. A number of people would be invited by their friends to stay for a weekend or longer in a country house or similar congenial place. There, in a friendly and welcoming atmosphere, they would be helped to real faith in Christ. But latterly, as the movement developed, it was too often merely to some sort of moral reform. They would be introduced to 'sharing'—the mutual confession of weaknesses, sins and personal problems—and to the 'Quiet Time' when they learnt especially to listen to God for guidance, often without much reference to the Bible. This sharing and confessing became particularly dangerous as the movement developed. Often shameful things were confessed in public, sometimes in the presence of somebody who was involved and could be seriously hurt by the confession. None the less, many found a new freedom from the bondage of *self* here, and a contemporary account described 'the gaiety and adventurousness of spirit of these groups', and 'the fellowship and laughter of our group meetings'. Thus Murray commented in 1922: 'Had a priceless time at Buchman's weekend house party, Cambridge, in August. It was a real tonic to me to be able to get there, and the only thing of its kind possible this summer, Keswick Convention, CSSMs etc., all being off the menu.' The atmosphere of early 'Buchmanism' must have suited Murray perfectly, combining as it did great seriousness with the light-heartedness and humour of the 1920s. The house parties clearly were 'lots o' fun', and more so when he was around. Murray's choice of guests was sometimes unconventional, as this anecdote shows:

> A down-and-out alcoholic had been in the Air force in the war. An excellent pianist, often playing with a row of drinks on the piano, he was living rough on the Embankment. He seemed genuinely to want the deliverance Christ alone can afford. I had been invited to a weekend house party, and told to bring anyone I wished. None of my hospital friends could come, so I invited my alcoholic down-and-out. I had to lend him a collar and tie, and after a shave he would have passed as a student. But on arrival at the house party I found it rather more posh than expected, with real silver at meals and many valuable ornaments around the house. I kept a wary eye on my companion—he had told me that he had been in prison more than once for stealing to get money for alcohol. But all was well. There *is* honour among some thieves at any rate.

Back at St Thomas's, Murray was working hard, studying for exams and ministering to the people of Lambeth. The following is his own account of those busy days:

> The poverty in Lambeth was truly terrible: damp and draughty tenement houses, some with rain pouring through the roof. Doing the "Midder and Gynae" [Midwifery and gynaecology] house job one saw the misery at first hand. I remember spending a night in a leaking bed-sitter where an enormous double bed occupied most of the long narrow room. The woman was too ill to move and there were no maternity flying-squads in those days.

An elderly 'gamp' was in charge, who had no nursing training but had acquired her knowledge from her mum, a local gamp before her. She must have weighed nearly twenty stone, and had to clamber across the patient's legs to reach the far side of the bed, which sagged almost to the floor under their combined weight. Buckets and basins were on and around it to catch the rain-water. I could not stop the gamp from talking about funerals with the terribly ill woman listening, fully conscious. Mercifully both mother and baby survived.

In the hop-picking season most of Lambeth migrated to Kent to pick the hops. Whole families went; it was their only annual holiday. I had spent another night in a home delivering a baby, went back to hospital for a bath and breakfast, then returned to see if mother and child were all right. I knocked and waited. There was a whispered consultation inside, then the door opened a crack and a suspicious eye peered through.

"Can I see Mrs …?"

"No, yer can't; she's gone 'opping'", and the door was slammed shut. After further consultation the door was flung wide open:

"Oh Doctor, we're so sorry. We didn't know it was you. We thought it was the gentleman come to collect the rent." How like some of us, when the Lord Jesus knocks at the door of our hearts!

The loyalty and kindness of the poor of Lambeth was a constant challenge and cheer. One pay-night when Casualty was full—accidents, wounds and drunks,—a harassed Mum brought in her small daughter aged six or seven, with both bones of the forearm broken: "Me 'usband come 'ome from the pub, drunk as usual, an' chucked 'er down the stairs. Can you fix 'er up, and I'll come back for 'er later. I can't leave 'im alone with the other kids." We had to give her gas, set the bones and put her arm in plaster. She never cried or murmured. When Mum came to take her home I gave her a bar of chocolate which I had in my pocket—one seldom had time for a meal on pay-nights. She took the chocolate, carefully wrapped it in a grubby hanky, and tucked it in the pocket of an even grubbier frock.

"Aren't you going to eat some of it now?" I asked.

"Wot! Me eat it now, wiv four little bruvvers and sisters at 'ome? They must 'ave their share, mustn't they?" It puts me to shame when I think of that child.

Doing children's outpatients I was unwise enough to tell a Lambeth mother that her small boy had gastritis and that she must have given him something that upset him: "You tells me I dunno 'ow to feed my children, an' me buried four!' The criterion of good motherhood was not how many reached maturity, but how many you had buried! And she went on, as she gathered up her offspring and marched indignantly out, "You say 'e 'as gas-tritis; if 'e 'as, 'e's in'erited it, 'cos 'is Dad died of gas-poisoning in France. So there".

The contrasts in a doctor's life are often extreme: a GP has to learn to "rejoice with them that rejoice, and weep with them that weep', as he passes from delivering a longed-for baby, to attending the death of a beloved parent. One of the cheeriest souls I met was an old and typical tramp—I had to peel his filthy socks off his ulcerated feet, and gently wash and bandage them. He had what he described as a "nasty 'ackin' corf" so I said,

"Take your coat and shirt off, Dad, and I will listen to your chest."

"It will take a long time, Doctor."

"Why?"

"Just you see."

And he took off his ragged coat, and proceeded to unwrap layers of newspapers from his emaciated body:

"Doctor, if you ever 'ave to sleep on the Embankment, remember, there's nothing like the *Evening Noos* to keep you warm in winter."

A little later I went to dinner with Frank Buchman at Brown's Hotel in the West End, popular with many Americans. After dinner he introduced me to other residents, among them King George of Greece and his beautiful, but so sad, Queen, a Rumanian princess. They were living in London in one of their intervals of exile. With them was the King's younger brother, Prince Paul. He and I had quite a long talk. I asked him if he had ever seen a big hospital at night. He said, "No, but I would love to". So we went down to Thomas's on the top of a bus, and I took him on my night-round, to one of the old long Nightingale wards of about thirty beds with the night staff-nurse sitting at the centre-table in the pool of light from the shaded lamp and the nurses moving silently from bed to bed. This picture always fascinated me. We watched an emergency operation from the students' gallery, and then we went up to my bed-sitter at the top of the hospital with its superb view of the River Thames and the lighted windows of the Houses of Parliament and Big Ben on the other side. Over a cup of coffee we talked, and after a short prayer together I saw him on to a bus at Westminster Bridge.

My friend Godfrey Buxton had hoped to go overseas as a missionary. Prevented by his war wound, he and his wife Dorothea now ran a "missionary training colony" in south-east London for men who planned to go abroad as pioneer missionaries: a tough assignment, and they were a tough bunch of mostly ex-service men. Every six months or so they ran a "drunks' drive" in a ramshackle mission hall near Clapham Junction, and I generally managed to join the team. We met on Saturday evening for an hour's prayer and were each allotted a pub. We made friends with the landlord and asked his permission to have a soft drink and chat to the chaps in the bar. At closing time we were all turned out on to the pavement, and our object was to take along to the meeting as many as we could. Some came, some refused. One man loudly proclaimed that he would become a Christian "when Tuck-Tuck-Amen's tomb was opened". What that had to do with it, he failed to explain.

We had to sing our congregation to relative quiet before the speaker gave a simple, short gospel message. A retired regular gunner captain began his talk one evening. "A year ago I was drinking a bottle of whisky a day…"

There was a very loud comment from the back, "Lucky fellah!" It was one of the most unorthodox Christian meetings I have ever been to; but God worked. One man, completely drunk, came forward to profess his wish to follow Christ and was visited a few days later. His wife said, "What on earth 'as 'appened to me 'usband? 'E 'asn't beaten me since 'e came 'ome on Saturday. 'E's different", and he appeared to be truly changed.

Murray always seemed to be at the centre of any activity. This was true of everything: of cricket, which he loved, playing for the hospital team often three days a week in the summer; and even more so of his Christian commitment. "When I first arrived at St Thomas's', he said, "There were no hospital Christian Unions; the London Inter-faculty Christian Union was, as it were, still in solution, but had not yet crystallized out. The half-dozen Christians who came to know each other at Tommy's met occasionally for prayer or a brief Bible-study in the hospital chapel.' A friend remembers Murray as 'one of the Cambridge men who revived the London Inter-Hospital Christian Union, which had been started in 1912 for Cambridge and Oxford medical students coming to London'.

When he could, Murray would join a group of Cambridge students and graduates camping at the Keswick Convention. It was while he was there in July 1923 that a telegram came to say that his grandfather, Prebendary Hanmer Webb-

Peploe, had died. As Murray put it, 'It was one of God's kind coincidences to take him to heaven during the Keswick conference where he had been a regular speaker for so many years.' Murray went to the funeral service at St Paul's, Onslow Square: 'On the coffin, and made of white flowers, was a model of a large open Bible and attached to it a card where my grandmother had written, "He learnt it; he loved it; he lived it." How true of my grandfather that was.

One might begin to wonder about Murray's studies—he seemed to expend so much time and energy doing other things. His contemporaries, however, seem unanimous that when he was working he really *was* working, and his good mind and memory helped. Feeling, as he did, that God was calling him to go abroad as a missionary doctor, he was concerned to be as widely trained as possible. Thus as well as his junior doctor post of house physician in midwifery and gynaecology, he also did a spell as house surgeon at St Thomas's, for which he obtained his primary fellowship. Indeed, he was offered a job as surgical assistant there but turned it down. Later he regretted not having spent extra time in order to obtain his final fellowship in surgery, which would have given him advanced operative techniques, but at the time he felt it more important to start working abroad as soon as he could. Thus he qualified with MRCS, LRCP in 1923 and returned to Cambridge to take the MB, B.Chir. degree in 1925.

In the New Year of 1925, Murray organized a skiing party at Wengen, in Switzerland. The party included an army friend, Hedley Glover; two of Murray's hospital friends, George ('Paddy') Metcalfe and Whitwell Hope Simpson; also Whitwell's sister Margaret (Peg) who later became Mrs Howard Somervell; two of the mothers of members of the party, Evelyn Webb-Peploe and Mrs Hope Simpson; and Dorothy Bradshaw, a cousin of the famous Studd family. While there, Murray and two of his friends had a remarkable adventure:

On a glorious sunny winter day we climbed the steep path above the village and descended to Grindelwald by the Mannlichen run, then returned up the railway track to the Scheideg. It was by that time dusk, and as we sat on a hotel verandah drinking hot chocolate,·we discussed the two routes down to Wengen. One was out in the open over the 'bumps'—snow-covered, scattered rhododendron bushes—good fun—and the other, longer, steeper and more difficult, a winding path through pine trees. I do not think as we sipped the 'schokolade' we consciously prayed for guidance, but we had as usual committed the day to God in the early morning. Being young and foolish we chose the harder and darker way. Suddenly, half way down, we came upon a teenage Swiss girl, weeping bitterly, a little boy by her side sobbing, and below at the edge of the wood a small girl with a toboggan, up to her waist in soft snow, utterly unable to climb back to the path. It was getting dark and freezing hard. One of us skied down to retrieve the little girl, the second took the small boy on his back; the third went ahead to meet the search parties. It turned out that these, with their nanny, were two children of a friend of my mother, Hugh Alexander, the splendid director of a first class Bible School near Geneva.

In her account of the same event, published under the title *D'ou vient le secours?*, the children's mother, as well as describing the prayers of the parents and of the children themselves in this crisis, tells us yet one more fact to make us wonder. Hedley Glover who was with Murray that day had himself had a miraculous escape as a small boy when he, his sister and their missionary parents fled 1,000 miles across China from the Boxers.[3] Now more than twenty years later, and an officer in the British army, he was to rescue two children of just the same ages, children of fellow Christians, lost in the snow. And apart from the rescue of the children, this adventure had a further consequence, leading, as will become clear later, yet another young man to give his life to rescuing children not in Switzerland, not in China, but in India.

In the midst of all his study, work, sport and Christian witnessing, Murray also managed somehow during his time at St Thomas's to run a scout group at weekends at Bracken Glen. Years later an ex-member wrote wondering if Murray could possibly be 'my old beloved scout-master', and remembering 'many profitable Sunday afternoons when we sang CSSM choruses and heard God's precious word from yourself and missionary friends.' The assistant scout-master was an old school-friend, Harold Ball. Murray had one of his amazing tales to tell about how their friendship was renewed:

> I was in my first year of clinical work at St Thomas's, and one morning in the Quiet Time the thought came to go across London and see a man I had been in the army with, and talk to him about Jesus Christ. I went across under the Thames in the little rabbit-hutch of an underground that shuttled backwards and forwards between Waterloo and the Bank. My friend was out. I was puzzled but left him a note, then set off back to the hospital. I was sitting in the little carriage at the Bank, waiting for it to start, when suddenly a man came sprinting down the platform, took a running jump between the closing doors, landed on the floor almost at my feet, picked himself up and sat down next to me. I turned to look at him; to my astonishment it was a man who had been at school with me—Harold Ball. We hadn't been in touch for four or five years. He told me he had just begun doing medicine at Bart's. It seemed he had nowhere fixed up to live, so he came and lived with my mother and me at Farnborough Park. Many years later he invited me to join him in his medical practice in Hampshire at just the right time. So what at the time seemed to be a mistake, turned out to be part of God's plan.

Like the Webb-Peploe brothers, Harold Ball was an excellent rugby player. While he was at St Bartholomew's, he and Godfrey Webb-Peploe used to play for the Harlequins 'A' side against a number of public schools. Sometimes they were joined by Eric Liddell, the Olympic runner and Scottish International wing three-quarter. Often after beating the school 1st XV, they would speak to the school Christian Union. No doubt they were listened to with respect.

One gets the impression that life was very hectic for Evelyn when Murray was at home. There were endless visitors. It was sometimes a little too much, and her health was 'not too grand'. But she adored her two boys, exhausting though they could be at times. Her grandson commented long after her death that she had, after her husband's death, only two interests in life: her faith and her two sons. In 1925 she supported Murray through a particularly painful trial: he had just become engaged to a delightful and outstanding girl, a Christian like himself, the daughter of a family friend. Suddenly and for no clear reason, she broke off the engagement. Knowing Murray's eagerness to see God's hand and leading in events, one can imagine that bewilderment must have added to his suffering of which Evelyn wrote to her cousin, Eunice Baker:

> I have suffered so much lately, on account of Murray's suffering—and must tell you briefly that he is not married, but his engagement is broken off. D. felt she had made a mistake as to her affection, and terminated it. She has suffered much over causing him such pain and sorrow—and of *his* suffering and pain I cannot write. I have been so overwhelmed by his side of it that I can still hardly write for the pain of it....We know nothing yet as to what lies before us.

But to Murray, shattered though he was by his broken engagement, the future—at least for the next year or two—was beginning to become clear.

6   China, 1926–27

It was only one month later that Evelyn wrote to her cousin
Eunice again. It was Christmas Eve 1925 and she was staying
with relations in London: 'Your news about going abroad is
not quite so amazing as mine. I am D.V. sailing for India
from Marseilles on January 9th with Murray on the *Leicester-
shire*, the Bibby Line. This has been an *extraordinary* and
wonderful leading out for me.'

Since he'd been about sixteen, Murray had felt that God
wanted him to be a medical missionary. It was for this reason
that he had changed from studying classics to medicine at
Cambridge. But as he was nearing the end of a six months'
stint as house physician in midwifery and gynaecology at St
Thomas's, he was puzzled as to the next step. This began to
become clear with the visit to the hospital of Dr Gordon
Thompson, a missionary surgeon with twenty years'
experience with the Church Missionary Society (CMS) in
China. He had just been appointed head of a hospital of 400
beds and a medical school in Hangchow—a large city about
120 miles south-west of Shanghai. He was home in England
on leave and looking for several new members of staff for the
hospital.

Murray recalled:

I felt at once that this was a man I would like to serve under, and
after meeting him the conviction grew that this was indeed the

72

answer to the need for guidance as to the next job. We had
several long talks and got to know each other better and I offered
to the Church Missionary Society to go to that particular hospital
under Dr Thompson. It was an unusual arrangement, in that it
was agreed that if for any reason he should leave Hangchow, I
would no longer be bound to the CMS—a point of crucial
importance, as things turned out, and clearly part of God's
overall plan of which we knew nothing at the time. The unorthodox proposal must have seemed an impertinence; however I
knew that the theological position of the doctors in these hospitals
varied quite considerably, and that I would only be happy
working with a man like Dr Thompson who accepted the Bible as
his authority and as the word of God.

When eventually they agreed to it in principle, the CMS sent
me to see two of their referees: one was a rather elderly and
churchy prebendary in London. I had been up all night dealing
with a maternity case and was not feeling too bright at 10 o'clock
in the morning, having had no breakfast and no time even for a
bath. He asked me how much I knew about the Prayer Book. I
said, 'I'm afraid very little, but I do read the Bible.' He said, 'My
dear boy, however can you convert the heathen if you don't know
the Anglican Prayer Book?' This was not a very auspicious start,
but after that, everything went fairly smoothly. So, while events
in Britain were building up to the General Strike, I found my
thoughts being turned to China.

Murray had probably hoped to marry before setting out for
China. Now, with the engagement broken off, his mother
suggested going with him—a suggestion to which Murray,
always conscious of his responsibility towards her, agreed.
This had in fact been the original plan before Murray became
engaged. Another reason for the idea seeming to be a good
one was that Murray's brother Godfrey, who, although four
and a half years younger than Murray, had not been held up
by war service or by lengthy medical studies, was already in
China. He had gone in the autumn of 1924 to work with the
Children's Special Service Mission (CSSM)—one of the first
people to be sent abroad by them. On the way he had spent
three months in the district of Tinnevelly, near the southern
tip of India, where he had 'come like a fresh breeze into our
midst straight from home'[1] and helped R. T. Archibald, also
of the CSSM, with some children's missions. (This 'fresh

breeze' picture seems a very apt one for Godfrey. He is quoted himself in the same CSSM publication as telling other workers among children: 'We cannot be of much use to God unless we are fresh through living in the presence of God.' Godfrey seems always to have had this 'freshness of the presence of God' about him.)

While in India, Godfrey had twice been 'to Dohnavur, to Miss Carmichael's nurseries for the Temple children—times of great spiritual uplift and refreshment. I had two days in their forest house right up in the Western Ghats with clear mountain pools for bathing, and the joy of God's life amid the forests and mountains ended my stay in India.'[2] He had then gone on to China as planned. Now it seemed clear that Murray also was called by God to China. Godfrey wrote home, 'I had almost given up hope of the family centre being in China, but perhaps it may yet be.'

As Godfrey had done the year before, Murray and Evelyn planned to stop off at Dohnavur on the way out. In the letter already quoted, Evelyn went on to explain:

> I had planned to be with a friend at Ramsgate this winter, but Dorothy's action in the termination of her engagement has altered my plans. Murray and I have decided to accept an invitation to Dohnavur in south India given to us *before* his engagement, when Miss Carmichael thought that I might be going out to China with him. She asked us to pay her a visit on the way out, so we have accepted; we had a cable from her a few days ago giving us a warm welcome.

This letter from Miss Carmichael to Evelyn, dated January 16th 1925, included the invitation to which Evelyn refers:

> My dear Mrs Webb-Peploe,
>   Your Godfrey is just about to leave us. I need not tell you what he is. You know far better than I the quiet depths of that beautiful nature; I can only say that constantly he reminds me of his Lord. Dear Friend, you are a rich mother. You have much to give.
>   When you go to China, as I hear you may, would it be possible to go via south India? It would be a joy to see you and Godfrey's

brother, and it would bind us all the closer to China—land of my
first desires.

    Lovingly and gratefully yours,
      Amy Carmichael.

Plenty will be learnt later about the Dohnavur Fellowship,
which was based in a small village in the plain, east of the
Cardamom Hills and some thirty miles from the southernmost tip of India. Suffice it now to say that Miss Amy Carmichael, a missionary from Belfast, had been working there
for almost thirty years and was building up something akin
to an orphanage, except that it was a Family and she was its
mother. The children were not literally orphans, but they
had been handed over by their families to serve in the Hindu
temples with all the evil practices which that involved, and
had in various ways escaped or been brought to Dohnavur.

Apart from Godfrey's happy experience there, Murray
had an additional reason for this visit, namely Dohnavur's
proximity to his friend Howard Somervell at Neyyoor in
Travancore, just across the mountains. Howard had been
working in England as a surgical assistant when in 1922, to
his delight, he had been chosen to take part in the first serious
attempt on Mount Everest. On this attempt Somervell,
Norton and Mallory had together reached a height of nearly
27,000 feet before being compelled to retreat. Before returning
to England, Howard had travelled to the far south of India
and had come to feel that he must dedicate his life to surgical
work in that poor and remote area. Back home he spoke of his
decision to Murray. He had found on reaching London that
his own hospital (University College Hospital) had offered
him a surgical post, which meant, as he put it, 'that the front
door to eminence in my chosen profession had been opened'.
It was difficult to turn down such an opportunity. He said, 'I
could see that the wrench was going to beat me if I didn't look
out, so I went to a friend who I knew would understand; I
told Murray Webb-Peploe, then at St Thomas's Hospital,
exactly how the land lay. It is somehow harder to shirk a duty
when someone else, whose friendship one values, knows all
about it.' So it was that Howard Somervell offered himself to
work at the London Missionary Society hospital at Neyyoor.

His one request was that he might be set free, if selected, to join a second attempt on Everest. He was, and in 1924 Somervell climbed to within 1,000 feet of the summit, returning to base camp to hear the news of the fatal disappearance of Irvine and his close friend Mallory.

Now that Murray, on his way to China, was visiting India for the first time, he spent a week at Neyyoor, taking advantage of the opportunity of doing a little surgical work with Howard. Then after three happy and busy months at Dohnavur, Murray and Evelyn travelled on to China.

Missionary work in China came as waves on the Chinese shore. It has often come and often been repelled: the Nestorians, the Franciscans, the Jesuits, the Protestants. From the sixteenth century China attracted both traders and missionaries. Sadly, as the Chinese did not fail to recognize, the 'foreign devils' did much harm as well as good, for from the late eighteenth century onwards British merchants shipped Indian-grown opium into China in order to pay for Chinese tea and silk. The refusal of the British merchants to co-operate when the Imperial government of China tried to suppress opium smoking led to the Opium War in 1840, and thence to the Treaty of Nanking which, in turn, by making foreign residence in China possible, opened up the way for missionaries again.

In 1844 the first CMS missionaries sailed for China, and in 1853 Hudson Taylor reached Shanghai, to start what eventually became known as the China Inland Mission. In 1867 he moved on to Hangchow, where two years earlier a CMS missionary called George Moule had settled—the first definite case of an inland mission away from a treaty port. It was here in Hangchow that Murray was to work. In 1872 an 'opium refuge' had been opened there, which formed the basis of the soon-to-become famous CMS medical work. Large new hospital buildings were opened in 1885, a leper hospital in 1892 and a women's hospital in 1893. Dr Duncan Main was in charge of the hospital and, in addition to the medical work, the gospel was effectively brought to thousands of Chinese by the evangelists and Bible women who talked with the waiting patients. A well-equipped medical school was opened in October 1924. It was greatly admired as being an outstanding combination of Chinese and Western architecture—Chinese in outward appearance, Western in its up-to-date interior and equipment. It was said that apart from the Rockefeller building in Peking, there was probably no medical school in the Far East so well built and equipped.

The year 1925 had been a difficult one at the hospital, with anti-foreign and anti-Christian outbursts and student riots. The medical college had to close temporarily, but reopened in the autumn with between fifty and sixty students; this was the situation, with Dr Gordon Thompson appointed to take over as superintendent from the retiring Dr Main, when in May 1926, at the age of twenty-nine, Murray Webb-Peploe arrived. He went at once to Hangchow, where he was welcomed by Dr Main, while Evelyn joined Godfrey in Nanking.

He recalled:

That month was spent leisurely learning the way around, mildly attempting the local variety of monosyllabic and explosive sounds which constitute the Chinese language, and doing a spot of surgery when there was occasion. Hangchow is six hours by train south-west of Shanghai, and is a walled city of well over 1 million people, including the suburbs outside the old city wall, which is now derelict or demolished. Beside it is the West Lake, famous throughout China for its beauty and historic associations, set in a half circle of low hills. (The inspiration of the 'Willow pattern' china is supposed to come from Lotus Island in West Lake.) The city has some fine broad streets and modern improvements, but much of it is as it has been since the Flood, I should imagine, and one sometimes thinks Chinese cities could do with another…

The hospital has 250 beds. The men's hospital block has nine wards, a good theatre, and the X-ray department. There is a new, well-planned outpatients' department with attractive circular 'moon' doorways, and a fine dispensary. The women's hospital distinctly needs a new inside; the maternity hospital could do with both sides new—in and out. Behind all the routine work of the hospital lies the fundamental purpose of the whole show, to share with the patients and students and nurses 'the priceless privilege of knowing Christ Jesus as Lord' [Phil 3:8; from the Weymouth translation that Murray liked to use.] Even with the amenities of civilisation in a so-called Christian country, a man whose body has been restored to health can utterly fail to find joy if his spirit has not found liberty and love and life. Far more so in China is mere physical patching, or even curing, likely to disappoint and dishearten.

Murray also mentioned in this letter that Godfrey was unwell and had to leave China temporarily. After a holiday with Murray in the hills at Kuling, he and Evelyn returned to Dohnavur for the winter.

Murray went on to the language school at Nanking. An older missionary lady commented, 'Poor Murray is now in China without either mother or brother. It is very lonely for him.' This seems to be merely conjecture, but remembering that Murray must still have been deeply saddened by losing his fiancée Dorothy, it may well reflect the truth. On the other hand, a letter to his mother written from Nanking gives the impression that here, as everywhere, he found plenty of contacts and friends: 'Certainly Nanking is a most interesting place for meeting people, and yet I am glad in a way not to be here long.' Perhaps he had in mind the same feeling that Godfrey had expressed in a letter earlier: 'Please pray that God may keep me *free* from the subtlety of the social entanglements that will abound in a big city like Nanking.'

Looking back over more than fifty years, Murray wrote this account of his time in Nanking and then in Hangchow:

The language school in Nanking was run most efficiently by Americans and Chinese. They did not worry too much about teaching you the Chinese characters—how to read and write—the idea was to become as fluent as possible with the spoken language. After three months one was able to get what one wanted, find one's way around and examine a patient—and even give a short talk on the wards with considerable preparation. It was one of the most efficiently run shows that I have come across.

In Nanking I got to know a number of Europeans and it was a very interesting time. At weekends I would try to visit some mission hospital within reasonable range. Travelling was fairly primitive; the carriages were unheated and the windows had been mostly smashed in various local wars, but with the hurricane lamp turned low tucked between one's legs and a good thick rug, it was possible to keep warm even in freezing conditions. The only difficulty was that at night one could not use the lamp both for reading and for keeping warm.

I started work at Hangchow at the beginning of 1927, but after only a few months we had to close the medical school and send the students home. It was one of the first occasions on which Soviet Russia had begun to try to export communism to other countries: the northern provinces of China were being ruled by independent military governors all fighting against each other, while Dr Sun Yat-Sen with others who wanted a strong republic unifying China had his headquarters in Canton in the south. The Russians offered to help him organize a northward expedition to crush the military governors. They sent a senior diplomat called Borodin and 400 Red Army staff officers to Canton. There they set up a training school for officers; then having trained a large number, they raised an army and started marching north. Soon the order reached us that all British nationals must leave Hangchow and concentrate with other British in Shanghai. We went to see the British Consul at the coast and asked whether my chief and I could remain on in Hangchow because we were very short-handed and the Chinese doctors had asked us to stay. He was a sportsman and said that he could not give us permission, but if we liked to stay on our own responsibility that was our own business. We decided to stay.

Soon after that we heard from a similar British mission hospital further south that the communist army had occupied the city and that they had hit on an excellent piece of propaganda to whip up the already fairly strong anti-British feeling. They had raided the anatomy school there and taken out the half dissected arms, legs and heads, put them on barrows with large placards: THIS IS WHAT THE BRITISH DO TO OUR BROTHER CHINESE—and then paraded them through the streets of the city. When my chief heard of this he said, 'We simply must not allow this to happen here'. We spent the next few nights burning our medical school's half-dissected limbs to prevent a repeat performance.

When the communist army entered our city, the hospital was full of wounded soldiers from the northern defending army. These poor chaps, knowing that if they were found by the communists they would be murdered, begged us to get them away if we could. We had to get them down to the station, load them on to goods wagons and send them off to Shanghai. We had one chap who had had a bullet in his spine and was paralysed from the neck downwards. He could not be sent away, so we dressed him up as a woman and put him in a small ward in the women's V.D. block, hoping he would escape detection. It was pathetic to have to send these poor chaps off, many of them with fractures and in great pain.

After the communist army had occupied the city, we kept quiet in the hospital most of the time, treating anyone who needed it, including wounded from either side. Eventually the Chinese doctors came to us at about midnight one night and said, 'We have reliable information that they are going to search the hospital in the morning; it is time for you to go.'

They had laid on a house-boat in a creek of the river outside the city, but the city was walled and the gates were shut and guarded at night. The doctors provided us with two reliable rickshaw men and said that our best scheme was to leave the city at dawn when the city gates would be opened, and just drive down the main street. At dawn the following morning Dr Thompson and I—he in the leading rickshaw—drove out of the hospital gates on to the main street which was swarming with Chinese communist soldiers. They began saluting us, and my chief called to me over his shoulder, 'Acknowledge all these salutes', and so all the way down the 5-mile road to the city gate and the river we were returning the salutes of the Chinese soldiers. We discovered later they they had saluted us out of the city as Russian staff officers, and then they shut the gates and hunted for the remaining British! They found none, for we were the last to get out of that city.

People sometimes ask, 'Do you believe those stories in the Old Testament?' I certainly do. There is a delightful story in the second book of Kings and the sixth chapter. The prophet Elisha had been doing an efficient job of secret service work for his country and the King of Israel. When in danger he prayed to God first to open his young servant's eyes to enable him to see God's chariots and horses of fire in the mountains round about, protecting them from the Syrians; and next to smite the Syrians with blindness to prevent them seeing where they were. God can still smite the enemy with blindness. I do not think that Dr Thompson or I had prayed this particular prayer, but we had certainly been praying throughout that week for both guidance and deliverance, and the Lord answered our prayers.

A few days after leaving the hospital, Murray wrote a letter for publication in England; clearly his brief spell in the East had not driven his beloved game of cricket from his mind:

We feel that we foreigners pulled out at the best time, after the inevitable disturbance due to change of government had calmed down, and before the agitators could begin seriously to affect anyone in the hospital. When we left, the side was not out, and we hoped to be able to return later to continue the game with friends glad to have been trusted and glad to have us back. We felt that the hospital could meet the anti-Christian storm better with the foreign scaffolding removed; our presence would only embarrass, and might actually endanger our Chinese friends.

They tackled their tremendous problems like Christian sportsmen, feeling the responsibility and facing the issues. It may be that they will have to close the hospital, for they, as well as we, realize that it is better to close with honour than to keep going with dishonour. Anyhow they will have had their innings; the wicket is sticky and the light is bad, but, win or lose, we ask you to join us in praying that they—and we—may play the game until the stumps are drawn.

    Yours merrily, in the peace of God,
      Murray H. Webb-Peploe.

A few days after they reached Shanghai, news reached them that the communists were attempting to take over the hospital from the Chinese Christians who were in charge. A leaflet was produced by the committee of the movement to take over the 'Kwang-Tsi' medical school. Roughly translated, it ran as follows:

Priests and preachers first, and then foreign warships and troops come against the smallest people in the world to possess the land and people, and make them their disciples, and increase their power. The imperial idea is creeping on, getting possession of property and finally establishing a kingdom. Imperialism is spread in China through the preaching of religion, this is their real method of capture. There is more than 100 years of history to show this. The most insidious method is education, so they eagerly try to establish schools. The English Kwang-Tsi medical school is well known for producing foreign slaves and followers. We have vowed to recover it, and so make a step towards overthrowing British imperialism.

In fact many of the students remained wonderfully faithful to Christ. In Shanghai, Murray was visited by a student who had remained in the hospital helping in the wards and so was there when the communists searched the hospital the day after Murray and Dr Thompson had left. As well as looking for any remaining British nationals, they were also set on arresting and punishing Christians. This student was arrested by the Communists; they had already turned the hospital chapel into a court room. The communion table became the prisoner's dock and he was set up on that with his arms and legs bound by ropes. They told him that if he did not renounce his Christian faith, he would be shot. He replied that he could never do so, that he owed everything to his Lord and Saviour Jesus Christ, and that they could do what they liked with him. There was a general uproar at this and a passing communist officer, hearing the noise, came in and said that the boy must be properly tried by the People's Court. In the meantime one of his friends had slipped up behind him and cut the rope and, in the confusion and discussion that followed the officers arrival, he escaped.

Murray spent a few months in temporary medical practice in Shanghai and then, as there still seemed no possibility of his returning to work at Hangchow, he went back to Dohnavur, initially for six months. He observed:

In many ways I was sorry to leave China. Even in that short time I had come to love the Chinese; they are a remarkable people. One very rarely saw a Chinese man doing nothing—a contrast to the situation in India. Life is hard, and they take the rough with the smooth—it is far more rough than smooth—with remarkable cheerfulness. It is probably never safe to generalize about people in any country, but it does seem that one of the basic characteristics of the Chinese is an underlying antipathy to foreigners of any kind. In Christ this can, and is, largely overcome; but it is as well to remember that there is this basic characteristic, understandable when the less fortunate results of their dealings with foreigners are borne in mind. At any rate, I had come to love and admire the Chinese, and was sorry to have to leave.

I had also enjoyed working with Gordon Thompson. I had had some fine C.O.s in the war, but I had never served under such a leader as he—calm in the confidence of God, and carefree in the certainty of his guidance. It had been lots of fun working with him in Hangchow, and a great partnership.

7 'Directed Service': The Call to India, 1925–28

In an undated scrap written to Evelyn from Dohnavur, probably around 1929, Amy Carmichael wrote about Murray and Godfrey, rejoicing in having them with her: 'Oh these two, what gifts to the world they are, worth all your life of loving sacrifice, worth anything—never have I seen two like them, it is rest and strength and comfort just to have them in the house.'

Murray has described 'from the Chinese end' how first Godfrey and then he himself, having been called to China, were forced to leave and went instead to India. There was much more to this change of direction than meets the eye, and 'seen from both ends' it seems to be one of the most remarkable events in Murray's whole story. Before delving more deeply into the significance of the move, it may be helpful to consider the whole question of 'directed service', which was one of Murray's favourite themes, and which he often expounded later to student groups and others as follows:

All who are committed Christians, who know that, as St Paul puts it, 'You are not your own; you were bought with a price' [1 Cor 6:19–20] because Christ died for them, want to serve him as effectively as possible. Clearly, though, one can either serve him haphazardly or else under his direction, and the latter should be much more efficient, much less wasteful of time and energy than haphazard, undirected service. If a man has two employees, he is going to get better value from one who comes to him for orders and does what he is asked, than from one who expends a great deal of energy doing things which do not in fact need to be done.

And so the question arises, 'How can I know the will of God?' Or, looked at from God's point of view, 'How can God get through to me and tell me what he wants me to do?'

Christians who have made, as Murray put it, 'a total committal of as much of myself as I know to as much of Christ as I know', can claim God's promise in Isaiah 58:9,11: 'Then you shall call, and the Lord will answer....The Lord will guide you continually' (rsv). And the way this is achieved is in what Murray called 'two-way prayer'. This is prayer that involves both speaking and listening. Thus in Luke 6:12, where Luke records that Jesus continued all night in prayer to God,[1] the Greek literally means that Jesus continued all night 'in the prayer *of* God'—a different pattern and direction. The idea is summed up in Psalm 143:8–10, where the Psalmist asks that God will: 'Cause me to *hear* your voice of love in the morning, Cause me to *know* the way wherein I should walk, Teach me to *do* your will.'[2] The last two requests speak of guidance and of obedience; the first speaks of the key factor in directed service: silence, listening—especially listening in the morning, before the busy day begins. Thus when King Solomon was told by God to ask for a gift, he asked (1 Kings 4:9) for an understanding or, as the Hebrew sense is, a *hearing* heart.

Similarly, in Habbakuk 2:20: 'The Lord is in his holy temple; let all the earth keep silence before him' (rsv)or, as Pusey, the Oxford theologian, has it, 'Hush before him, all the earth.' And here Murray used to quote Pusey's comment, 'And to the hushed soul, God speaks.'[3]

This really is the key to directed service and, as Murray explained;

When God "speaks", it is the *thought*—the inward thought of God which comes to us. You don't hear a voice—I've never heard a voice, although occasionally I think people do. In the Bible, the phrase most often used is authoritative: "The word of the Lord came"...to Jeremiah, to Ezekiel, to whoever it was. The Greek word used here in the Septuagint version is *logos*, a word which can mean both the outward expression of the inward thought and the inward thought itself. Thus "the inward thought of God came..." and so it does today.

As a young officer in the army, I used to go in and salute my Commanding Officer, the Colonel. I did this every morning—in a dug-out or a shell-hole, wherever we were, I would go and salute and say, "Good morning, Sir; have you any special orders for me today?" Sometimes he would say, "Yes, do this, that or the other." Another day he would say, "Just carry on." And we must do this every morning of our lives (or some other time of the day if the morning is quite impossible, as perhaps for a mother with young children)—come quietly, hushed, into the presence of our Lord and ask: "Lord, have you any special orders for me today?" The name of a friend might come to mind, for whom we should certainly pray, and possibly also visit, write to or ring up.

The military image of a man coming to God as a soldier comes to his commanding officer may seem remote to us today. However, it is biblical: St Paul uses the same image of a soldier on service in his second letter to Timothy (2:4). For Murray, who fought in probably the most harrowing war the world had ever known, it was an image that came naturally —as it would to his contemporaries.

Murray was aware that there are grave dangers in this approach to guidance, although he certainly would not have advocated the sort of Christian living in which one merely drifts, sitting back and doing nothing unless prompted by a special thought from God. His own life was the complete reverse of this, every day utterly purposeful, not a moment or an opportunity for service wasted. For Murray—who was eminently sane, disciplined, completely honest in his dealing with God, and gradually becoming more and more experienced in and responsive to God's thoughts—this way worked beautifully and brought much glory to the Father; but most of us must tread very carefully if we seek to follow. In particular, Murray stressed, how are we to be sure that an 'inward impulse' is indeed from God, and not from ourselves, or even from the devil? It is vital to check the prompting by the word of God (the Bible) and also by the law of love. He pointed out that if to obey what seems to be a thought from God means letting down a friend, it can't be right. Also, circumstances should confirm the thought—we should see

God working through circumstances, 'working at the other end'. Experience helps and makes one more sure in recognizing genuine thoughts from God. The difference between a raw recruit and an experienced soldier is that the latter has absorbed the ideas of his commanding officer, and with time will come to know almost instinctively what to do in a given situation. Similarly, an experienced employee will not need to consult the boss over every small detail of the work. The better the Christian comes to know his Master, the more readily he will recognize his voice: 'Then shall we know, *if* we follow on to know the Lord' (Hos 6:3, AV).

To illustrate the process or mechanism by which God makes his will known to his servants, Murray used to expound the story of Peter's rooftop vision at Joppa (Acts 10) leading to the conversion of the first Gentile, Cornelius. This is a very remarkable story and Murray, using the alliterations that helped him to remember his points, picked out from it several ways in which God reaches out and makes known his will to man: *supremely* by prayer (Peter was praying, supremely the situation in which God can guide); *surely* by the word of God, *certainly* by the Holy Spirit, *sometimes* through other people, *simply* through circumstances and timing (the timing in this story was crucial, as the messengers would have had to be sent off the previous day) and *safely* by God working at the other end. This last was one of Murray's favourite themes, and is striking here. God could see both ends, and sent Peter and prepared him to give exactly the message that Cornelius was ready for. These principles of 'directed service' were vividly demonstrated in the way in which God called Godfrey and Murray Webb-Peploe from China to India during the years 1925—28.

The 'Indian end' of the story took place in the mission community at Dohnavur where Amy Carmichael, aged fifty-seven in 1925, was mothering, with the help of a team of Indian and European workers, a large and growing number of Indian girls and boys. Since 1901 when the first little girl, Preena, aged seven, of her own accord ran away to the Christians from the temple woman who was bringing her up for a life of religious prostitution, Amy Carmichael had been mother to such children. Checked in her first hope of going to

China, she had gone out initially to Japan in 1893 as the first
missionary to be supported financially by the Keswick
Convention, to work with the Reverend Barclay Buxton at
Matsuye. After not much more than a year, she had had to
leave Japan for health reasons, and in 1895 she set out for
south India to work with the Church of England Zenana
Missionary Society.[4] Soon she met the dedicated missionary,
Thomas Walker of Tinnevelly, and lived and worked with
him and his wife for some years, collecting round her a band
of Indian women who became known by a Tamil name
meaning the Starry Cluster, and who travelled and preached
in the area round Pannaivilai where Amy and the Walkers
lived. Gradually she became aware of the peril of the little
girls who were 'married to the god' under the Hindu *Devadasi*
system, and longed to rescue them.

What happened was that baby girls were handed over by
their parents to serve in the Hindu temples. As they grew up,
they were trained in the ritual dances of the *devadasis*—dances
with religious significance but also of strongly erotic character. As Nancy Robbins puts it, 'By her early teens or maybe
sooner a girl would go through her initiation ceremony of
marriage to the god; from then on she would be compelled to
live the life of a prostitute under the specious guise of divine
service.'

By the end of 1901 Amy had moved to Dohnavur; slowly
the family began to grow as one after another baby girl was
rescued from the temples, and a nursery was built. By 1906
the family numbered seventy, and by 1913 it was 140. More
buildings were constructed to house the growing family, and
often just when it was needed a money gift arrived to make
this possible.

A different trade in children of either sex, just as dangerous,
was associated with the drama companies that preceded the
modern cinema industry. This made apparent the need for a
home for boys as well as girls. In 1918 the first baby boy,
Arul, was brought to Dohnavur, and although it was clear
that if a boys' work were to begin extra leadership would be
needed, a boys' nursery was built, so that by 1925 there were
about seventy boys as well as all the girls, and a mixed team
of Indian and British workers numbering thirty-four. To this

large family Amy Carmichael had always been 'Amma' (from the Tamil word *ammal, 'mother'*), but there was no one with the necessary gifts for leading the boys, and no adequate medical work.

In the last chapter we saw how Murray's brother Godfrey, on his way to China in 1924, had stayed at Dohnavur. In her book *Gold Cord*, Amma described him at this time:

> Nine years later (after Amma herself had first seen small boys serving as acolytes to the gods in a temple festival) a young Englishman on his way to China climbed a hill overlooking one of the famous temples of the south. It was evening, and the beauty of the view, black mountain peak, dark forest, reddening sky, rice-fields spread like a green carpet, water falling in white masses into a deep pool, held him in the silence of worship. Suddenly the stillness was shattered. Drum and flute and wild clashing cymbal told of the evening pujah beginning in the temple. And a great rush of pity, and more than pity, for the polluted children bore down upon him. And he cried to the Lord of the children. And the Lord spoke to him there—told him that the task was hard, told him that he waited—but for whom? How should he know? He did not know. He was not told then, so he went on to China, nor dreamed that it was for him that the Lord was waiting; nor did we dream of what was being prepared for us and the boys.[5]

It was shortly before Godfrey left, in January 1925, that Amma wrote the letter already quoted, inviting Evelyn and Murray also to visit Dohnavur on their way out to China; and in April she wrote to Evelyn again, a letter that shows that the possibility of Murray being called to Dohnavur was already in her mind. After writing of the need for a doctor, she concluded, 'God guide you—Godfrey tells me that many voices are calling his brother, and I would not add to them. You will tell him about this open door if you are led to do so…In any case may the word come from God alone.' We do not know whether Evelyn mentioned it to Murray or not. At any rate, he pursued his plan to go to China, and from now on an intense spiritual battle began for Amma, in which her mind told her that Godfrey and Murray were to work for God in China, but her spirit seemed to be telling her otherwise.

The first phase of the battle concerned Godfrey, and here it is remarkable from notes that both he and Amma independently preserved that although she was in India and he was far away in China, God seemed often to speak to them simultaneously. Thus in the first week of July 1925, when Amma was unusually anxious about the spiritual leadership at Dohnavur, Godfrey noted this in his private diary:

A time alone with God. "Are you willing for something deeper? Will you give me a free hand with your life? It is going to cost. It means just this—I want you to follow me unquestioning." A sense of something impending in my life, a big change, a great test, or what, I cannot say. "O God, prepare me, mould me, get absolute possession, for Jesus' sake, Amen."

It did not immediately become clear to Godfrey what this 'free hand' would entail, and over the next year or so he continued his work and language study in China, his ministry reaching not only the Chinese, but also Western ex-patriate children. Among these was Cathy Nicoll of Canada who, as we saw earlier, met Christ through Godfrey there.

Meanwhile, on January 30th 1926, Murray and his mother arrived at Dohnavur on their way to China, as Amma had invited them to do. Murray's first impressions of Dohnavur are beautifully described in a letter he wrote to friends in England:

March 15th 1926. I wish I could take you with me to the compound of joyous children at Dohnavur, on the preaching trips to isolated villages in an indomitable Ford, across the paddy fields by starlight and hurricane lamp to a serious case in a village some miles away, into the outer courts of Hindu temples under the guidance of one who has been long in India and whom even the Brahmans trust and respect, and who also preaches Christ to them even in their own temples. The mystery, the magnificence and the misery of Hinduism sweep in upon one as one sees the lights far up a dark forbidding corridor where "the god" is being worshipped with the weird sound of the conch shells and the throbbing of the tom-toms.

They stayed until April, but while he was there Murray did not sit back idly and rest, conserving his energy for China.

He at once rolled up his sleeves and got to work. A small operating theatre had recently been built at Dohnavur but, as some new doctors had had to leave for health reasons and only Dr May Powell was left, the theatre was not being used. However, with Murray's arrival, Amma was able to report, 'Dr Webb-Peploe and our Dr May Powell are having field-days. The little theatre is in use for the first time. While the doctors were at work this morning, Koruth—a "Syrian" [or St Thomas] Christian from Kerala now working at Dohnavur—was in prayer for them in the Prayer Room, a tall white figure kneeling upright in the shadowy little room.'[6] Murray proved himself a perfect children's surgeon, joking with his small patients, blowing bubbles for them to watch while the anaesthetic took effect; and yet, as an Indian member of the family commented, 'fighting for his patients as a tiger fights for her cub'.

Murray accompanied Amma on preaching trips too. Here is her description of one of these 'glorious raids on the kingdom of darkness':

> We were engulfed in mud, and Murray Webb-Peploe was exceedingly muddy for he had been pushing the Ford out of a hole in the road and had been spattered with mud from head to foot. Of course a crowd had gathered and we could not pass on and leave the people without a word, so Murray jumped on the step and holding out his muddy hands called them to look, which they very much did. Then followed what they could not help understanding however dense they were, the blessed gospel of cleansing, illustrated by those muddy hands.[7]

Amma commented that she would always remember this episode for the 'mixed fun and earnestness' of it—a phrase that describes Murray perfectly.

Amma gave another vivid picture of these months of Murray and Evelyn's visit:

> After dinner when the things are cleared off the table, and only the flowers and lamps are left, we generally hearten ourselves after the long hot day with a song...and lately we have taken to reading for a little while together too, and while he was with us

Dr Webb-Peploe sometimes gave us the food on which he had been feeding, straight from his little well-worn Greek Testament, and somehow it was always the food that was convenient for us.[8]

Evelyn had been given the Tamil name 'Aruthal', meaning 'comfort', because of her knack of giving just the word that ministered comfort even when she was not fully aware of a person's immediate need. As Murray and Evelyn's joyful visit drew to a close, Amma wrote this: 'God bless that dear mother and her two sons who have been more to Dohnavur than we can say. To the most loving One who sent them our thanks rise now, for he knoweth whereof we are made and he is very kind to his poor dust.'

With Murray and Evelyn's departure for China, Amma's spiritual struggle intensified. She had begun to see clearly that Godfrey and Murray were exactly fitted to meet the needs of her family—Godfrey to lead the boys, Murray to build up a hospital and medical work. She had begun to see them as Dohnavur's St Francis and St Luke, although in her diary she asked, 'Control my prayers. Let me not covet my neighbour's goods—nor his men-servants. Murray and Godfrey are China's men-servants. Lord, help and forgive.'

Nevertheless, on September 23rd, after long waiting on God for direction, she paid the first advance for the land that became the boys' compound. And the very next day, as Amma heard long afterwards, Godfrey—far away in China —realized that because of poor health (he had rheumatic fever) he must leave China, temporarily at least. He decided to go to Dohnavur, and arrived with his mother in October.

On the very day, October 8th (and possibly the very hour, allowing for the time difference), when Godfrey on board ship on his way to India noted in his diary: 'Borne home upon me that I may never return to China…and God has work for me in India', Amma had a remarkable vision. This occurred while she was staying with some of the children at the Dohnavur family's new house at Cape Comorin, the southernmost tip of India and for centuries a centre of pilgrimage. The new house had been named Joppa because, as Amma explained in *Gold Cord* (p.261–2), 'We wanted it to be a place of heavenly vision for all who stayed in it.'[9] She described what happened vividly in a letter written five years later to Murray:

> On the night of Oct 8th 1926 I was sleeping out under the stars on the sand at Joppa. For a long time I lay listening to the sea, and about midnight fell asleep to be awakened almost at once by a sense of light and joy that words cannot show. I had seen you and Godfrey with me in Dohnavur. Dreams have no conscience. I was not conscious of any thought of China's loss or yours. It was just joy and light. Afterwards I pushed the thought away as a mere dream. The Lord had come to me that night on the sand under the stars—and I feared to recognize him, and told no one.

On October 23rd, Godfrey and Evelyn reached Dohnavur from China: as far as anyone knew, just for a visit until Godfrey's health improved. So Amma noted, 'Under everything through that happy day was an urgent cry—"Lord, let not my heart even look towards him with wanting feelings. Keep it detached."'

On October 28th Amma called an extra prayer day at Dohnavur. Godfrey noted that during the day God seemed to be calling him clearly to resign from the CSSM and offer himself to the Fellowship,[10] and so on November 14th he wrote to the CSSM tendering his resignation. It was two days after that that God himself seems to have reawakened for Amma her 'Joppa' vision; thus she wrote to Murray in the letter already quoted, that:

> the word on November 16th came as a startling shock. It woke me before dawn: "You have never asked me for Murray and Godfrey for the future leaders of this work." I said nothing for I was troubled. And he said, "Why have you not asked me?" And I said, "O my Lord, you know why I held back my heart from asking." And he said, "Ask me now."
>
> But I did not mean to mention it, and could not understand why I suddenly did—and reproached myself much—especially when I saw Godfrey's startled eyes. At least they seemed so to me; such a quick surprised glance could only mean, I thought, the presumptuous sin.

Here we have a word of explanation from Evelyn: 'Miss Carmichael told me and Godfrey what the words to her were, 'to ask', but *we* could not tell *her* he was going to offer until he heard from the CSSM—accepting his resignation.'

Thus God's word to Amma came two days after Godfrey had written to the CSSM. No wonder Godfrey looked startled, but his lips were sealed until the CSSM replied. He commented in his notes for November 16th 1926: 'God's word to Amma in the early morning, confirming my call. How good he is!'

Having been told 'to ask', Amma obeyed; costly, breaking prayer, sustained only by faith. At last she noted, on December 15th 1926 at 6.35 a.m.: 'Turned into joy. Godfrey offered for the work.' She observed, 'For half an hour I was where time does not count and there are no words. There is such a thing as being silent in joy.' And on the back of her notes on the guidance she wrote this: 'I looked up Godfrey's dates to see if they were marked dates here. I think the result was very solemnizing: 'Take off thy shoes from off thy feet— that is how I feel as date after date shows God's hand upon us all.'

It was now 1927. There was no respite for Amma in the spiritual conflict: at this moment Murray was finishing his language studies in Nanking and was about to begin the medical work at Hangchow to which he had been called. Amma prayed on, still not clear as to how to pray, conscious of a spiritual battle going on around her. She told Murray later, 'There was a day when I did not know how to bear it. The powers of darkness closed down upon me.' But, as so often, the Lord met and strengthened her with an encouraging word, this time from 2 Samuel 7:18–29 (where David contemplates how far the Lord has brought him already, and what great things God has promised him for the future).[11]

The course of God's bringing Murray to Dohnavur, already described from his end in China, can be followed through letters written from Evelyn in India to her cousin Eunice:

> *Undated scrap*: I had a cable from Murray the other day, sent out on Feb 26th [1927] saying that "all arrived Shanghai", and that he was well. We saw in the *Madras Mail* that all Europeans

had left Hangchow *except two doctors* before the entrance of the
southern army.

June 27th: Dohnavur: just back from the Nilgiris—the Blue
Mountains. Murray, who has six months' leave, came there to
see me for a week-end on his way to Dohnavur. Should Hangchow
reopen to the "foreigner", Dr Thompson will cable for him to
return at any moment, as he is remaining in Shanghai to watch
over developments and care for hospital matters.... Godfrey is a
different being in health, and looks strong and well now. I am
thankful that he is out of China for good.

July 19th: Murray has been very busy medically, relieving Dr
May Powell during his "leave" from China. So far the situation
in Hangchow is such as to close the hospital to any foreign
doctors.

Murray had reached Dohnavur on May 31st 1927—thus
May 31st became known as Murray's Coming Day. These
special days had been introduced for the children at
Dohnavur because often their birthdays were not known;
however, the adults were given them too. Of Murray's Coming Day, Amma wrote later, 'How well I remember the hour
after we had said good-night, and I sat up in bed and read
Daily Light; the last words of the morning reading, "Blessed is
she that believed: for there shall be a performance of those
things which were told her from the Lord" [Lk 1:45] and of
the evening, "For all the promises of God in him are yea, and
in him Amen, unto the glory of God by us" [2 Cor 1:20]. I can
feel the thrill of them still.'

As Evelyn said, on arrival Murray started work at once.
There was no proper hospital then, and medical work was
done in a part of the old buildings set aside for the purpose.
As far back as 1921 Amma had felt strongly the need of 'a
Place of Healing, furnished with all that was required for the
help of the people, its work led by one in whom were the
instincts and convictions and the glad abandon of the spiritual
pioneer'.[12] She and May Powell, who joined the Fellowship
in 1924, were both praying for the man who would plan and
build this hospital, and lead its work. Thus it was a happy
day, when in August 1927 the first gift of £100 arrived for the
building of the hospital, and Murray was there and led them
in thanks. Amma described the scene vividly in *Gold Cord*

(p.282): 'I see it all again—the dancing blue-clad children, the forest bright with orange and crimson leaves, the tall trees on either side, the tall man leading our thanksgiving. And he who led us was he to whom, in the counsels of God, the leadership of that which was now at last begun was to be committed.'

However, at this stage there was still no reason to suppose that Murray would be able to stay in India, although by December he had still had no word recalling him to China and it seemed that the communists were still holding on to the hospital in Hangchow. In January 1928, Amma described, using the phrase that Murray himself loved, how the Fellowship met and 'in that living silence that can only be when the Lord is near, we hushed our hearts before him'. The Lord spoke through the reading of the crossing of the Jordan and through the letter of a friend. They were sure that God wanted them to go ahead and buy land for the hospital, and still surer when more money came.

Eventually in the spring of 1928, God spoke to Murray, notably in the early hours of March 3rd, as he was waiting at Madura station for a train. The way in which it became clear to Murray that he was to stay in India is recorded in his own private prayer diary, in which he noted down special requests he made to God on particular dates, and also anything it seemed that God was saying to him as he came quietly to him early in the morning before the busy day began. The relevant entries are as follows:

> *Feb 4th 1928: Daily Light*: "Ye shall henceforth return no more that way."
> *Mar 3rd*: 3 a.m. Madura station roof. Freedom to do this sort of thing—to go into the wilderness at the call of the Spirit.
> "Your work is here."
> "Fear not, I have called thee."
> Isaiah 46, especially verses 9, 10 and 11: "I am God…my counsel shall stand, and I will do all my pleasure: calling…a man that executeth my counsel from a far country: yea, I have spoken it, I will also bring it to pass."

These notes for March 3rd throw light on what Amma later called Murray's night of ordination. She referred to it in a letter written to Murray on March 2nd 1941: 'The night of your ordination, Murray, beloved. If the word came to you after midnight, then it belongs to March 3rd. Either way, it is one of the days never to be forgotten, for on that day I saw a light on your face that told me, before your lips did, that you had spent a night with God.'

However, even after his night of 'ordination', Murray had to wait patiently a little longer for the situation to resolve itself. His prayer diary for the next four months shows clearly how this happened, both through God speaking to him in his daily readings and ('from the other end') through Dr Gordon Thompson's decision to leave Hangchow. Although the hospital in Hangchow was eventually handed back to the CMS on July 1st 1928, Gordon Thompson had by then accepted another post—that of surgical director to the Henry Lester Institute in Shanghai—and this, under his original agreement with the CMS, ended Murray's contract. Murray received news of Dr Thompson's decision on July 4th. On July 5th he read yet again in *Daily Light* the verse that had repeatedly spoken both to him and to Amma throughout this time: 'Blessed is she that believed; for there shall be a performance of those things which were told her from the Lord' (Lk 1:45). He cabled that day to China, 'Orders clear—India. Request release.' Gordon Thompson's reply, 'Send resignation London. Loving regrets' came a week later, and Murray noted, 'Amma opened by mistake, so told all.' It was on that day, July 13th, that he wrote a brief and always to be cherished note to Amma, 'May I stay here? Murray', and on July 14th he was welcomed as *sonthum* (their own) in the Dohnavur family. So at last the battle was over. Amma's joy was reflected in letters written to Evelyn at this time:

Dear dear Mother of Murray—He's *sonthum*,
    You know it—you know what it means of heart's joy too deep for words just now. I have tried to write but cannot. I can only say this and leave you to understand.
    In joy, the greatest that could have come on this side of heaven, and in grateful grateful love,

                                                          Amma

And also:

It is all beautiful, the sure leading. "It must come from the other end", he said, and often I wondered how it possibly could. Now it has, I ponder it all, turn over every step in the wonderful ordering of events and worship God—I don't know anything as humbling as an experience like this.

We had a thanksgiving service at 11. None of us found it easy to put our thanks into words, I least of all. I blundered through somehow but so poorly that I could only look up and say, "Lord, please understand without words, for they won't come." I don't think they ever will come in full till I have learned the speech of heaven.

8 Missionary in a Mess: India, 1928–31

The Indian countryside to which the Webb-Peploe brothers had now returned from China is dominated by the spectacular Western Chats. Dohnavur lies at their foot in the red earth plain, where men's livelihood depends upon rice crops grown in brilliantly green paddy fields edged with palmyra palms.

From his arrival in 1927, Murray had immersed himself in the study of Tamil, the language of the south. An Indian friend, V. Thyaharaj, has described how 'he put his whole energy into learning the language. Besides, he learned dozens of stanzas of the caste people's "bible", the *Thiru Kural* of Thayumanavar. People were delighted to hear and see a foreign doctor able to talk effortlessly with them in the colloquial tongue.' In fact, although Murray's excellent memory enabled him to learn Tamil and its proverbs with comparative ease, his complete lack of musical ear meant that his pronounciation was always poor, and in this respect Godfrey's Tamil was far superior. Godfrey was interested in the language for its own sake; for Murray it was primarily a means of reaching people. And this he undoubtedly did—he had the ability to reach across to people of an utterly different culture and to relate to them simply as one human being to another. Thus Thyaharaj has recounted the beginning of his own friendship with Murray; a delightful account that shows a sensitive, intelligent boy of the East testing out a Westerner and finding him worthy of respect and love:

In one of the early books written by Amy Carmichael, *Meal in a Barrel*, there is a fine picture of Murray sitting with a bunch of youngsters sorting out articles just unpacked from a huge box. If photographs depict their subject's character this picture certainly does of Murray, an attractive strong young man in his thirties. One young person, neither attractive nor photogenic, not to be seen within the camera frame, was concentrating his thoughts assessing this foreigner.

The young person of course was Thyaharaj himself. He continued:

Early in 1928 Murray took a bunch of young men on a climbing spree. They were camping in the mountains for about a week. Down in the temporary 'hospital' this same Indian teenager was ill and in a critical state. A message was sent to Murray. Within half a day he was alongside the boy, who asked to be baptized. It must have been the first baptismal rite Murray ever administered in India. Something clicked between them and a friendship began. What a friendship between two people of such extremes! Murray more than fifteen years older, with many academic achievements and accomplishments; in contrast the young Indian with nothing but his scanty formal education and his heritage of Indian culture. Yet their friendship was not based on "I'll be your friend as long as it serves my purpose." Many a foreign missionary inevitably has in the background an Indian trailing along with him, but such a spirit was detestable to both of them. They came to know each other intellectually and spiritually. They could argue with and contradict each other. A few years later, following the young man's recovery, they happened to spend a short holiday together—just the two of them. One day, after their Bible study, Murray said to his friend, "We two are like David and Jonathan. God has given you as Jonathan." That was Murray.

Largely through his friendship with Murray, Thyaharaj eventually expressed his wish to become a doctor. From then on Murray gave him coaching in anatomy and in other pre-medical subjects, but because of Amma's early policy of educating all the Dohnavur family children in the unrecognized family schools, he was only able to train as a pathology technician, a field in which he became very competent. Sadly, he never received the medical training he longed for; instead he became the man on whom everyone in the hospital leaned for spiritual counsel and for practical support, eventually receiving state recognition as a doctor, on the ground of his long experience.

As early as 1927 Murray was acquiring a circle of patients in the nearby small towns: the Saivite town of Kalakkadu ('Joyous City'), Tirukkurungudi ('Holy town'), famous for its Vaishnavite temple with its centuries-old sculptures, Eruvadi ('Song of the Plough') with its Moslem community of weavers and merchants, and many others. In Tirukkurungudi in the autumn of 1927 Godfrey spent a month learning colloquial Tamil, getting acquainted with the people and their culture, and dispensing medicines and dressings with occasional supporting visits from Murray. 'Yesterday's excitement apparently was that I wore a *veshti*, he wrote. 'As long as they realize one is human, that's good enough for the first week!' That autumn too Mahatma Gandhi was touring the south and once Godfrey went to hear him speak. While agreeing with much that he said, he prayed that Gandhi's eyes might be opened to see 'how far the eternal outweighs the temporal. Oh that he might know Christ, for he has no message of eternal life to all these people who listen to him'. In March 1928 Godfrey was described by Amma as 'up in the Forest now, with some forty-five boys, studying Tamil and taking Bible classes. He's enjoying the birds of that glorious place so much [fairy bluebird, jungle babbler, whistling schoolboy, emerald dove] that mealtimes are much disturbed as yards of him hang over the verandah as he climbs about to get a good view of them.[1]

Meanwhile, amid the pressures of language study and the joys of busy outpatient work, another unexpected instance of God's guidance occurred in Murray's life. He recalled how early one morning—the date was March 15th—in his Quiet Time, he was reading and then praying over one of the prayer letters from the Officers' Christian Union (OCU) that he regularly received. It reported that two of the members would be coming out in the autumn to visit officers at the military stations in northern and central India. 'I prayed, as asked, for these two chaps,' he said, 'then quite out of the blue it seemed as if God was saying to me, 'Are you willing to be one of them?' But I said, 'Lord, they've got two already, and they don't need a third—and besides, I shouldn't leave the work and language study here.' But I made a note, with the date, in my Quiet Time diary.' Indeed he did, and the entry can still be seen: '15.3.28: "Are you willing to be one of the OCU mission group in India?" Yes, but let it come from the other end.'

This was always Murray's determination: not to choose and blindly pursue his own course, but to wait patiently until what seemed right to him was initiated also 'from the other end'. Thus a month later there was this entry: '27.4.28: OCU mission to India, Hebrews 10, verses 35–37. *Daily Light;* patience, promise. ("Ye have need of patience, that, after ye have done the will of God, ye might receive the promise.")'

Two months later Murray received a telegram from the secretary of the OCU in London: 'Can you join Ruby Wright tour military stations in northern India October to March next. All expenses met. Great opportunity. Letter on way. Forster.' And Murray noted in his prayer diary that day: '27.6.28: Cable from Col. Forster re Indian tour. See 15.3.28 Q.T.'

He waited nearly a month before replying:

> I looked at the telegram and then I took it across to the skipper of our mission, Miss Amy Carmichael, saying "My first instinct is that I can't possibly do it, as I don't want to interrupt my Tamil studies, or to leave the work here." I also showed her the note in my prayer diary. She said, "This seems to be of God; let's pray about it." Indeed the whole Fellowship prayed. Miss Carmichael told me later that she had asked the Lord whether, if I was to go, I could somehow continue my study of Tamil—the ideal would be to have a Tamil-speaking servant who also spoke Hindustani, the language of northern India.

The story was amusingly taken up by Amma herself, writing in the *Dohnavur Letter:*

> We were getting near the time when Murray must go and no one had turned up. "It's a tall order, you know", Murray said. Somehow fresh faith was born at that moment, and next morning I stayed in and got on with work in my room, so as to be at hand

when the Impossible appeared. At 9 a.m. there was a call from near my verandah. A tall soldierly looking man, a regular ruffian he looked too, stood upright and saluted. It was a magnificent salute, the kind that uplifts you.

"Salaam, Amma."

"Salaam, younger brother; what is thy desire?"

"I desire to join the honourable family of Amma."

"But what canst thou do?"

Silence; he was pondering the question. "I might be a night-watchman," he said at last.

"Dost thou talk Hindustani?"

"For eleven years I have talked that language."

He was soon in my room, and after another of his wonderful salutes he condescended to sit down; you can get nothing out of a Tamil until he is at home enough to sit down. He told me of his life—he had been a soldier in the Great War, had seen Lord Kitchener, had fought under Sahibs. He liked army ways, army discipline, Sahibs, white men who did things "krect".

"Were you ever orderly to a Sahib?"

"I know how to give a letter," and up he sprang, saluted, made as if to give a letter, stepped back two steps and stood at attention. I told him of a Sahib who was here, a soldier (his eyes gleamed), a captain in the Great War, a very good and noble Sahib. I called Murray from the dispensary, and the Ruffian took to him at once. A few days later his new master had the joy that is above every joy, he led his servant, Utthaman, to the feet of our Lord.[2]

While Murray was awaiting clear guidance about this tour as 'missionary in a Mess', there had been minor excitements to enliven the routine of his busy life. For instance:

One morning *chota* [the light early breakfast] was disturbed by a scared and breathless youth bursting in with the cry, "My uncle has been bitten by a tiger!" The uncle was duly dealt with in the dispensary; then followed a delightfully typical scene at the "field of battle" where, with officials writing reports in triplicate, the tiger not surprisingly gave his hunters the slip. But the wounded man was truly converted to Christ and later invited us to proclaim the gospel in his village, which thereafter became known as "the village opened by a tiger".

Also at this time, a policeman who had become a magician was led to seek Christ at Dohnavur. He brought his charms with him and they were dramatically burnt during a service in the House of Prayer. Murray always felt that the conversion of such a man had to be accompanied by the total destruction of all the tools of his trade.

In August 1928 Godfrey became gravely ill with rheumatic fever. 'There were days to live through then', Amma recorded, 'that I thank God are past.' While he was ill a new worker arrived in Dohnavur—John Risk, an English ex-naval midshipman with a miraculous story of God's working to release him from H.M. Service so that he might take on some of Godfrey's heavy work-load. Amma told how 'for weeks before he came Godfrey was working at a new Tamil study plan for him which will prove of great value to all our new students. He has made a little grammar and some direct method study cards, based on what he learnt at the Chinese language school in Nanking. I wonder if there ever was a more fruitful illness.'[3] But its effects remained for many months. A sad letter written to his mother in December shows how great were the pressures on both him and Murray, and how truly humble they were. (Different though the brothers were, their response in the following situation would have been identical):

Your letter of 26th came an hour ago, and, Mother dear, you need never be afraid of telling me the truth. I deserve everything you said, and I really don't know how to ask your forgiveness because it was the absolute limit not to make time to write to you for Christmas. The only excuse I have will perhaps help you to pray for me, knowing the truth. Sickness *never* seems to draw me to God, as people write in many holy books; it has the exact opposite effect on me—the devil seems to have much more power in temptation and to pray seems more difficult, and what with another dip of fever and my toothache I'd about reached the limit. I know that's all human and wrong; I know only too well what I ought to be and do, but I'm just not what people are kind enough to think me.

I did try on my birthday to give you joy by coming down from Naraikkadu and it cost me quite a bit physically the double journey—and even then it seemed I did it the wrong way, because I didn't let you know beforehand. Mother dear, I do try to show I love you sometimes; do help me by prayer that I may do it better. I know this Christmas omission was inexcusable, so please forgive and pray that I may live close enough to the Lord not to fail you and not fail the boys here.

Ever so lovingly, Godfrey

This letter makes it seem that perhaps Evelyn was becoming difficult. Perhaps she was finding it hard to accept the fact that Amma was now becoming closer to her sons in some respects than she was. At first she had lived at Dohnavur, but for health reasons she soon spent more and more time up in the cooler climate of the Nilgiri Hills. Murray and Godfrey visited her when they could, and both wrote to her regularly, at least once a week, taking her into their confidence and sharing things with her for prayer.

Murray was at hand for the worst part of Godfrey's illness, then at the end of October he set off on the OCU tour. The new chimes in the recently completed House of Prayer rang out each hour to remind the Dohnavur family to pray for them, as Murray and Leslie ('Ruby') Wright set off to cover '10,000 miles of extraordinary interest and wonderful hospitality'. In less than six months they visited thirty different military stations, staying usually only two or three days at each and doing all they could to strengthen and encourage the Christians among the officers they met.

From 12th–20th November Murray was at Meerut, and while there he received a letter from CMS accepting his resignation. He was then free to write to Amma at Dohnavur, offering to take over the leadership of the medical work and, as she commented, 'our Unseen Leader had given him the charge of leadership'. This may seem puzzling in view of Murray's note of July 13th to Amma, 'May I stay here?' and her rejoicing the following day, 'He's *sonthum*', but it will be remembered that Amma's opening a cable by mistake had necessitated Murray's asking her prematurely whether he might stay at Dohnavur; otherwise he would no doubt, like Godfrey, have said nothing until after his resignation had been accepted.

From Rawalpindi he wrote in December to his mother:

About eight officers, young, keen, smart and good at their job—and out to witness. Just the right work for a good nucleus; it's splendid, for this and Peshawar are two of the key places on the

North West Frontier. Met Brown, son of old gym instructor at Shorncliffe. Also met Sgt Major Gingell. He still reads his Bible daily; hope he goes all right over Christmas—there's an awful lot of drunkennesss then in the army—very little at any other time. It's a tragic way of celebrating the Lord's birthday.

Pray for Utthaman; he's sulky because I had to tick him off for going out in my Burberry raincoat—he has my old one already, but I suppose he thought mine was smarter and he didn't think he'd meet me! He's pretty lonely up here. A line from you would cheer him a lot—he prays daily for you.

Kohat, 14th Jan '29: I wish we could have longer in places. Many hungry folk have to be left apparently high and dry, but the Holy Spirit can and does, I am sure, carry on.

On January 20th he wrote from Razmak asking his mother to pray for various people whom he had met: 'A Miss Fisher (staying with an Air force officer's wife) who was a musical comedy actress is really thinking—very struck by Ruby's life on the boat coming out. She may come to Dohnavur en route for Colombo. I must get a special sanction for my strange friends to come, short skirts and all.'

And on February 21st he wrote from Poona: 'Life is very interesting. Am *very* happy, and also very fit; much fitter than when I set out.'

Towards the end of the trip they were in Bangalore and here Murray met somebody who later became a great help to the Dohnavur family—a trained engineer called Philip England:

Actually I met him at a rather drunken guest-night at the Madras Sappers and Miners Mess. There was one Christian officer in the Unit, and he invited me and my friend, together with this Christian civil engineer in the town. The result was that Philip England was called by God to join our mission and he came and built our hospital. He was a tremendous asset. So you never know what God is doing. Not many missionaries get their call on a drunken guest-night in the army!

So the OCU tour was a great adventure and immensely worthwhile. It was work at which Murray excelled. Amma described their exuberant return to Dohnavur: 'If you had been there you would have seen battalions of boys skirmish-

ing about, all keen to be the first to hear the hoot of the horn
that told of Murray Annachie's homecoming. Soon the lorry
came tearing in with a flourish of hoots and shouts from the
whole community.[4]

Once back, Murray wrote to his mother remembering her
birthday: 'It is good that you are so much better. You are
very precious to Godfrey and me, and we can never repay
your outpoured love and sacrifice. You always give yourself
and do it to the point of pain. Pray that I may learn more of
that giving.'

So Murray was back at Dohnavur. With the letter from the
CMS freeing him the last obstacle had been removed; for the
next eighteen years he was to throw all his energies into
serving the community at Dohnavur, where both he and
Godfrey were also to give themselves, joyfully and in their
different ways, to the point of pain.

Murray got down at once to medical work and to planning
the new hospital. We have already seen how in January 1928
the Fellowship had unitedly become certain that God meant
them to go ahead in faith and buy land for the hospital. One
by one all the little plots around the periphery were bought
before the central plot was secured. The man owning this
was asking a ridiculous sum for it when 'the impossible
happened. The surrounding owners began to jeer: "Have
your cows wings that they can fly over to your portion in the
middle?" and no one likes to look ridiculous. The middle plot
came to terms at last, and we walked over it singing in our
hearts.'[5]

One day late in 1928 Amma had chanced to be in the
bazaar of a Hindu town. Suddenly a big burly stall-keeper
exclaimed, 'I hear you are going to have a hospital at
Dohnavur. You will make it a paradise.' Amma was delighted
with this remark, and she commented amusingly, 'Our first
hospital was not in the least like paradise. It was a hen-
house—Buckingham Palace, we called it.'[6] Subsequently, a
nearby Indian house was turned into a little pro tem hospital,
the Suha Vasal, or Door of Health, but by the spring of 1929,
with Murray back from his tour, plans for the new hospital
began to be drawn up. Amma recorded in the *Dohnavur Letter*
that 'on the evening of April 30th 1929, the first plans drawn

to scale lay on the table before us'. Who actually drew these plans? Certainly Murray did most of the planning at this stage: 'Can you imagine the intense interest of the sketches Murray is making in odd corners of time? Line by line it is being given; all the intricate thoughtfulness required is of God as much as anything else.'

Amma delighted to tell this story about the choosing of the hospital's name:

> We had invited the leader of the gentry of these parts to come and talk over the Indian thought about the hospital arrangements, for Murray wanted to consider not only what the West approved, but what the East felt about the matter.
>
> "For the name, how does *Parama Suha Salai*, Other Health Place, appear to you?" we asked, and the stately old Hindu smiled his benignant smile, "Doubtless a beautiful and perfect name, but not quite fitting for our hospital."
>
> "Kindly explain the thought that you are thinking."
>
> "The thought that I am thinking is this: those words imply spiritual vision, and therefore the other-world health which follows upon spiritual vision. But is it not rather upon the good medicine to be given that we should direct the thoughts of our patients?" We told our friend how exactly he had described just what we wanted. "Then *Parama Suha Salai* is the one perfect name', he exclaimed, "The Place of Heavenly Health!"[7]

Amma's reference to Murray making sketches in odd corners of time was of course accurate. There were many demands upon him, but first priority had to go to his work as doctor and surgeon. It seemed that at this beginning of the project everybody's eyes were upon him, and the reputation of the hospital at stake. At the end of May he performed a particularly dramatic operation, which did much to ensure his reputation. A young Indian woman had developed an enormous ovarian cyst and was borne down by what her old Christian mother described as a 'burden as big as Christian's in *Pilgrim's Progress*, only his was on his back and hers in front'. In the West such a thing would have been dealt with much sooner, but here it served to emphasize the need for a small hospital in this rural area. The woman herself was very peaceful as Murray led her relatives and the theatre team in praying for her. When the bells sounded many of the family also prayed, and after the heroic task of its removal was completed, Murray returned to the recovery room to give thanks. The cyst proved to weigh thirty-six pounds, most of it fluid, being more than one-third of the woman's total body weight, and in due course her relatives and others were shown it and the story spread around. 'He has a mighty god,' they reported, 'and he walks with his God, and that is why these wonderful things are happening.'[8]

Another day Murray operated on a cow that had been gored. The operation was performed by the steps of the theatre, with crowds of interested people watching from a suitable distance. A big basket was put over the cow's face, and Sister Erna Struwe administered chloroform. The wound was successfully repaired, and the grateful owner drove the cow away!

Murray wrote for the *Dohnavur Letter* at about this time an account of a doctor's day that makes one tired simply to read it. Among other things he described:

> the hospital prayer-meeting, a real live show, with the patient who is to be operated on joining us. His old father who has come to attend on him, and whose one and only garment looks as if it hadn't been washed since the Flood, potters into the theatre after him. (Horrors!—I know; but one learnt from a surgeon in China the value of allowing in a relative or two while an operation is going on.) We pray before starting, and a group of the children come and sing Tamil lyrics and joyful hymns outside the theatre until he is under the anaesthetic, a real help to us all. Part of the bone has to be sawn off, and all the diseased tissue. It is a long job, and longer because it is the first time the operator has ever done it.

This 'doctor's day' ended with an interruption while Murray was reading up on the anatomy of the neck in readiness for a tumour operation next day: 'In trotted an agitated hurricane lamp and behind it the local Indian CMS padre. A young man who had been employed by him was apparently mad: "He is indubitably a crack. We apologize for these many botherations at this time of night." I tried to sort things out, and so to bed after reading, "Great peace have they which

love thy law: and nothing shall offend them [Ps 119:165]."'
Indeed Murray wrote to his mother at about this time: 'Well,
God has wonderfully fulfilled a promise claimed on reading
Daily Light for June 4th 1927, in the train from Tuticorin: "In
this place will I give peace, saith the Lord" [Hag 2:9], and he
has.'

In August 1929, Amma, Murray, Godfrey, John Risk and
some others went up to Naraikkadu ('The Forest') where
high among the mountains, the Dohnavur family had two
holiday houses. They were going to rest and to concentrate
on language study. A group of girls went at the same time to
stay with Evelyn in the Nilgiri Hills. Murray, Godfrey and
Amma all wrote to Evelyn at this time, and their letters gave
a picture of great happiness:

From Amma, Aug 30th: If I wrote for a week I could not tell you
what these days have been. I can never get to the end of what it is
to have Murray and Godfrey both together here. We have most
peaceful joyful times, and much good Tamil work is being done.

From Amma, Sept 9th: Murray and Godfrey are pure joy, and my
dear John too. We are very happy, but I wish I could do more for
Murray (Godfrey needs nothing I can give)...but Murray has
Godfrey. [A mysterious and perceptive comment this, which the
reader must interpret for himself.]

Also from Amma, Sept 16th, commenting on a Tamil paper she had set:
Godfrey's was almost perfect and Murray's simply amazing; if
only he can get time he will be great at Tamil but he must have
time.

From Murray, Aug 25th: I hope you are as happy and as well as
we are! Last night was one of the most wonderful nights I have
ever seen—a moonlight rainbow bright silver against the
mountains and the sky.

From Murray, Aug 30th: John arrived today and so we three go
up to the Top House, leaving Amma in peace. We shall come
down for a bathe, tea, Tamil with her and dinner below and then
back up Top for bed. Godfrey is getting new birds and enjoying
himself. We soak in Tamil pretty well from 8 a.m. to 8 p.m. so it is
very valuable being up here.

From Murray, Sept 8th: Yours, Mother, is a real ministry, having
six of the family up there. They must be having a great time.
Godfrey is extremely fit. God is marvellously good to have
brought us three together in one place like this. I do thank him

for Godfrey as a partner, he is a joy all the way.

At the beginning of October, Philip England, the engineer whom Murray had met at Bangalore, came for a visit and helped Murray with the hospital plans. They discussed various points, such as whether electric lighting should be introduced into the whole compound, or just in the hospital. They decided on the latter. Murray wrote to his mother, 'Philip has been working at the theatre plans and has got out a splendid rough plan for us. It will cost a lot; but if the plan is right, that will come.'

One evening back in June, as Murray was driving Amma in the Ford, he had suddenly thrown out to her this question: 'Brick in lime, or mud and thatch? Which should it be?' Several of the earlier buildings had been built of mud and thatch and had suffered both from white ants and from ill-wishers who set fire to the thatch. The answer to Murray's question, and to the more general one of the standard required throughout the hospital, came in a verse that Murray noted from his reading on August 16th: 'The house that is to be builded for the Lord must be exceeding magnifical' (1 Chron 22:5, AV). He took these words as setting the standard of workmanship for the hospital; not that it should be grand in any way—far from it—but that it should be good or, as Amma put it, comely and suitable for its purpose.

In his 'Quiet Time' up in the Forest, early in the morning of 2nd September, Murray felt constrained to ask God for £1,000 in one single gift for the hospital. He noted this request in his prayer diary; the thought had just come 'out of the blue'. Fifteen weeks later, on December 15th, during Amma's birthday celebrations, a cable arrived announcing 'One thousand pounds for maternity ward'. Amma described how they met together in the big schoolroom and 'thanked our Father, and rejoiced with the children who loved their Doctor Annachie'.[9] Later Murray received a letter from the donor telling how in the week beginning September 2nd she had felt God constraining her to send £1,000—an enormous sum of money then, and one that took all her savings. The gift was taken as God's sign at the outset of the work that the Fellowship had not been mistaken; the hospital was assuredly in his purpose. Nevertheless, its detailed plans at this stage were constantly being modified and improved. The list of things necessary, given in the *Dohnavur Letter* of April 1929, included the following:

> A caravanserai for the relatives and their bullock-carts and animals; an isolation block for lepers; temporary quarters for very superior secluded people who won't mix with ordinary mortals. They need a little place where they can stay and a little kitchen where they can cook, uncontaminated by even a passing glance; private wards—little houses where a whole family will camp with the patient—each with its own kitchen and little back-yard; kitchens—one for each caste; a whole new scheme of sanitation.

In addition, of course, they needed all the usual structures and equipment of a working hospital. Quite remarkable too was God's provision of the engine needed to drive the dynamo that would provide electric power for the lighting and X-ray plant. Just when they were needed, two such engines became available at a greatly reduced price because they had been used for two nights only to provide special illuminations for the Viceroy's recent visit to Travancore. Who but God himself could have timed that 'coincidence'?

So Murray worked on, throughout 1930 and into 1931, with medical work, Tamil study, evangelism and the planning of the hospital. His vision for this last was given in a small booklet where he stated that he hoped that it would be 'a place where people would come, not to be preached at, dosed, and dealt with as cases, but to feel at home, to watch, thaw, to allow those who take their names and wash their bandages and dress their wounds to tell them what the Lord Jesus has done, and can do for them'.

Amma wrote in the *Dohnavur Letter* of December 1930, describing a baptism service, and saying how she was set free to pray because the actual business of the service was being undertaken by others: 'Godfrey and Murray think of every minute thing and carry everything through in unbroken peacefulness, each brother fitting into the other like the notes of a musical chord.' And at the beginning of 1931, with the nurseries expanding steadily, the boys' work established, and the hospital foundations being laid, Amma gave serious thought to the future leadership of the work. Bishop Houghton described how 'on January 17th, when Murray was away and Godfrey ill, she gathered all who could come in God's garden, and found that they were of one mind with her. Did it not appear that God was preparing Murray and Godfrey to be leaders on the men's side, and May Powell on the women's side?'[10] (At a similar meeting some time earlier they had agreed that Arulai, one of Amma's earliest Indian co-leaders, should lead the women's work. Possibly her poor health gradually precluded this. She died in 1939.)

On February 8th Amma and Murray were driving to Kalakkadu and the question of the future leadership came up. Amma made it clear then that she envisaged Murray eventually becoming the overall leader of the work. Dr May Powell comments, 'Murray's humility was such that he thought the overall leadership would be my responsibility. I was in the car with them when this was cleared up and I realized then how wonderful that, with his gifts, he had been prepared for a woman leader.'

Murray worked on into the spring of 1931. A Canadian nurse, Margaret (Evalda) Sutherland, joined the Fellowship at this time. She has recalled:

> The building of the PSS was already well in hand when I arrived. I can remember going out with Amma to look at the partly finished buildings and foundations. This was a time of progress and enthusiasm in every area of the work and a very active part was taken by Murray. How enthusiastic he was to use any new Tamil phrase he had learned and how ready to quote a Tamil verse—usually a new one each day—as he made his rounds. He was also very ready with a Tamil proverb to resolve a difficult situation and produce a smile of agreement. Murray lived at this time in a small bungalow beside the Suha Vasal (Door of Health) which had easy access both to the people from the village and to those in the home compound. It can be imagined the constant strain on one of Murray's friendly nature to be so easily available both day and night.

Indeed, by now Murray was exhausted; also, there was a need to recruit new people for the hospital team. Thus it was decided that Murray should return to England for a while.

9 Leave in Europe, 1931–32

Of Murray's time in England Amma wrote: 'I have called it furlough, but the word is absurd in that connection. He is out on campaign and having glorious times with our glorious Leader.' In fact Murray now launched on a year that could perhaps be compared to the phrenetic last burst of a Catherine wheel, except that it occurred in the middle of his life of service and not at the end.

Even his few days spent in Colombo on his journey home were used by God. A man from Eruvadi called Silavudeen (a name familiar to Westerners as Saladin) was in Colombo working to pay off a debt. By birth a Muslim, he had already spent some time at Dohnavur and had turned to Christ there. Knowing that Murray was staying at the YMCA, he called to see him, wondering what sort of a reception he would get. 'Everybody looked so grand in their English clothes and I came just as I was from my work,' he told his friends later. What happened amazed him. 'There in front of all those grand people Murray Annachie puts his arm round me and welcomed me as a brother!' In today's multiracial society this might seem unremarkable, but in India in 1931 Murray's spontaneous action expressed clearly to this man God's supernatural love. When later Silavudeen returned to Eruvadi, fierce persecution of his family began and they were forced to leave their village and take refuge in Dohnavur. He and his wife became valued workers and witnesses for Christ in the Fellowship, but the immediate result was that Eruvadi, which was a Muslim community, proclaimed a boycott on Dohnavur and for a long time no one from there was allowed to attend the hospital.

Murray continued on his journey and reached England on June 6th 1931. 'Marvellous journey—many openings' he recorded in his diary. When he arrived in England he acquired a second-hand car, an Austin 12, and one of his first visits was to the Keswick Convention, the annual gathering of evangelical Christians that had given inspiration to the young Amy Carmichael and to many others and at which Murray's grandfather had been a well-known speaker.

At Keswick, on 18th July, Murray met a striking young Dutch woman with fine aristocratic features and long black hair that was coiled into a bun. She was Oda Baroness van Boetzelaer, who had trained to be a missionary nurse at Mother Eva's community, Friedenshort, in Upper Silesia. Mother Eva herself was highly born; she was brought up in the castle at Friedenshort. Coming to Christ at the age of seventeen, Mother Eva had dedicated her life to him and to the service of the poor. Interestingly, her missionary zeal was originally inspired by visiting England and hearing Prebendary Webb-Peploe speak at Keswick in 1905, and later, her Sister Deaconesses, trained at Friedenshort, went as missionaries to many parts of the world. Oda van Boetzelaer, whose parents were good friends of Mother Eva, had already offered for work at Dohnavur, and had come over to the Keswick Convention with a friend. She was vivacious, dedicated, and highly intelligent. Murray talked with her and her friend and was deeply impressed.

Wherever he went while in England, Murray had his eyes open for possible recruits for the new hospital. The hope was to have a team ready, trained and speaking Tamil, by the time the hospital opened. Thus a newly trained nurse from St Thomas's Hospital, Edith Hope-Gill, whom he met at Keswick in July, was in Dohnavur by November.

Keswick over, Murray began travelling round the English coast visiting the CSSM beach missions, talking and showing lantern-slides about the work among Indian children, and looking out for possible recruits among members of the CSSM teams. In the bright sunshine of an English summer he felt more full of vitality than he had for some years; and without realizing how hard he was pushing himself, he began to rush faster and more hectically around the countryside, talking quickly and earnestly wherever he went. His diary is filled with hasty reminders: people to see, to write to, and to pray for; group meetings. Occasionally the note appears, 'Speak slower, speak less'; and a diary entry is even made at 4.20 a.m.

In August Murray joined the CSSM at Cromer on the Norfolk coast; he had been invited as their missionary speaker. Here he met Hugh Evan Hopkins who was leading the CSSM and who was due to join the team at Dohnavur in some months' time. Canon Evan Hopkins has recalled his first impressions of Murray:

> I had never met anyone quite like him—so approachable and yet so obviously earnest. He was delightfully human. He came in with a kind of Christianity we hadn't seen before—free and easy. This was the Oxford Group—but of course he already had the heart of the matter before he joined the Group. I did become scared when I realized later from other people's warnings how 'Groupy' he was, as we were all at that time deeply nervous of this movement. Groupy Christians were always good at getting on with hard-boiled and worldly people. Thus the parents of my fiancée, Margaret Adamson, were very averse to her joining me in Dohnavur—not because I was not approved of, but because their lifetime in Singapore had made them feel that missionary work was a waste of time and energy. It was Murray who, by calling on them, enabled them to see the other side. They had the greatest admiration for him as a person, and eventually gave their full consent to Margaret's going abroad, although her father was still so upset that she had to do all her packing in the basement of her house well out of his sight. Murray's winning personality was hard to resist.
>
> It was at Cromer that an episode occurred that demonstrated how literally Murray carried out the Oxford Group emphasis on listening to God. In his case it was absolutely genuine; he walked very close to God and put to shame those of us who found difficulty in following Buchman's way.

Murray carefully recorded this story, as follows:

After three very happy days with the house party at Cromer, sharing in the beach services and the fun and games with the young, I was due to go on to Criccieth, in North Wales. I had allowed two days for the journey in my rather unreliable old car. Various things delayed me, and it was about midday before I finally set off. It was one of those lovely English summer days, and I was driving along a fairly deserted road about 6 miles out of Cromer and praying for various people as I drove. Quite suddenly out of a blue sky there came the arresting thought: "Stop and go back."

I pulled the car in to the side of the road, switched off the engine and asked the Lord why. I more or less said, "I'm late already in getting off, and have a long way to go. What does this mean?" It was one of the most vivid impressions of this sort that I have ever had, and the answering thought to my question was even more strange: "Go back to Cromer and ask Mrs Bulpitt if you can give her and her two children a lift to Birmingham."

I had met the two children, a girl and a young boy, also their governess, at the beach mission services and sports, but I had never met their mother. She was not in the least interested in these things and had just packed them off to the CSSM to get a bit of peace and quiet. They had told me that they lived in Birmingham, that they were due to go home at about this time, and that their father was there. I had no reason to suppose they needed any help, and this thought by the road-side was disturbing, to say the least of it. I began to argue with God, just as Peter did when he was confronted with the vision at Joppa and the order to do something that he had never done in his life before. I said, "I can't go and call on a woman I have never met and ask if I can drive her and her two children half across England. It simply isn't done." But the impression was so strong and one knew that God sometimes does these things and that the right thing is to obey. So I turned the car round, went back to the hotel where I knew the family was staying, and asked to speak to Mrs Bulpitt. When she came down, I began to explain that I had met her two children at the beach mission and that they had told me that they were due to return to Birmingham about now. I then said, "I am going to North Wales and have to pass through or near Birmingham; might I have the privilege of giving you all a lift home?" I don't know who was the more embarrassed, she or I, but she did what any woman would: began to give every possible excuse why she would not accept the offer: "My husband is not here. We've made arrangements to go by train", and so on. And then she added, "And anyway, my daughter is not very well this morning."

I said, "I am sorry to hear that. Have you had a doctor?"

She replied, "No, I don't know any doctor here; I'll wait and see how she is."

I said, "I happen to be a doctor and my job is mainly the care of children; would you like me to see her?"

She said, "I would be most relieved if you could."

So I followed her upstairs and found a girl of thirteen in bed. She had an almost normal temperature and pulse but she was slightly tender on the right side of her abdomen. After examining her carefully, I came to the conclusion that she probably had a very early acute appendicitis. I took the mother outside and explained that I was simply passing through, and therefore must call a GP in the town. I happened to know a good man, who came straight away but decided that there was nothing serious the matter. We disagreed about this and were talking about it when the mother came up and said, "I've been thinking things over, and in case my daughter should need any further treatment we would be most grateful to get back to Birmingham as soon as possible. My husband is there; we have our own doctor and if necessary a surgeon who knows the family, and a nursing home we could put her into."

I said to her, "Well, the car is at the bottom of the stairs; if you'd like to pack up, we'll get there as soon as we can."

So in twenty minutes they had packed everything up, and we installed the girl—her name was Millicent—on cushions on the back seat. Her brother had gone off the day before to stay with a friend. About every hour I stopped and took Millicent's pulse. It was ten faster each hour, and about an hour out of Birmingham her pulse rate was 120 and she was beginning to look a little grey. I was afraid that if we didn't get moving fairly quickly the appendix might rupture before we could get her operated upon. I rang from a call-box to arrange for the bed to be ready and for the surgeon and family doctor to be there so that we could operate as soon as possible, should the surgeon feel that this was the right thing.

They were quite splendid, and she was on the operating table within a short time. The surgeon asked if I would like to assist, and I said, "Yes, very much." When he had opened up the abdomen and fished out an appendix on the point of bursting, he looked across at me and said, "You've driven this child half across England; what's the story?" So I told him what had happened, and he said, "Well, I agree; this is the hand of God."

By this time the father had turned up at the nursing home. He was a wealthy industrialist, I discovered later. He invited me to their home for the night and, after supper, standing up against the mantelpiece in his drawing room, he asked me what had happened. So I told him, and he said, "Yes, I agree; God is in this." Then he went on, "You know, I haven't done much about God—I've been too busy making money, I think—but it's about time I did."

I said, "I quite agree."

And he said, "What do I do?"

So I explained to him quite simply that he could ask the Lord Jesus Christ to come into his life and be his Saviour and Lord. And that night he did.

The next morning I had to go on in order to fulfil my engagement at the Criccieth CSSM, having first rung up the nursing home and found that Millicent was doing well. The family invited me to stay again on my way back, an invitation that I gladly accepted. I reached Criccieth with not a moment to spare, having had a breakdown on the way. How I thanked God it had not happened the day before!

Three weeks later, therefore, I stayed with Millicent's family again. She had made an excellent recovery and was back at home; at her bedtime I was asked to go up and say good-night. I went up and she greeted me warmly and said, "I've heard such funny stories about you and me; what actually happened?" So I told her the whole story, and added, "I think that the Lord Jesus Christ saved your life that day", and she agreed. And then I asked her whether she would like to ask him to come into her life and be her Saviour and Lord. She said yes, she would, and so quite simply I explained to her how this could be done, and how Jesus is knocking at the door of our hearts, waiting until we will ask him to come in. She truly responded that night to the knock of the Lord Jesus Christ and has believed in and belonged to him ever since. Later on she ran a children's service at her local church, where some 100–120 children used to come.

Thirty years later this remarkable story was to have an equally remarkable sequel, as we shall see in a later chapter.

For the remainder of the summer of 1931, Murray kept up his hectic travelling. However, by now he was suffering from severe headaches, and also beginning to find it difficult to sleep, often waking in the early hours of the morning. He was very tired. Scribbled among endless lists of names—people to see, write to and pray for—come the words in his diary 'loneliness—weary. Burden to myself'. Again and again he wrote: 'Talk less; listen more. Lord, forgive and help.' On September 10th there is an entry made at 3.15 a.m.: 'Lord, the body? Sleep? A crash would dishonour your name. Lord, is this right, going round England, little rest?'

All through the September entries, intermingled with notes of jobs to be done, are signs of stress and prayers for help: 'Lord, fitness and strength please; no head. Can I go on like this?' Often too there comes an answering thought: 'My strength is made perfect in weakness [2 Cor 12:9]. You must get more sleep. Book no more meetings at present.' 'Lord, do you really mean no more meetings than already planned or promised?' 'Yes, I do.'

At the beginning of October Murray went to Holland, partly for an Oxford Group house party in Amersfoort. Also, Amma had asked him to visit the families of as many Dohnavur recruits as possible, and among the new nurses from Friedenshort was Oda van Boetzelaer. Oda came from a well-known Dutch family. Her father, Baron van Boetzelaer, owned a large estate with several farms. Oda's brother Charles was a close friend of the Dutch royal family, and she too had been to tea at the Palace as a little girl. Her true name was Thoda, itself a shortened form of Theodora, 'gift of God'. From childhood she had shown high spirits and a passionate love of animals. Her family were dedicated Christians. In 1922 her father had invited the Indian Christian preacher Sadhu Sundar Singh to visit Holland. Through this link and through their friendship with Mother Eva, Oda now felt called to serve God as a nurse in India.

Altogether six sisters from the Friedenshort Mother House were soon going to Dohnavur, and Murray spent time with them all, sharing with them some of Amma's ideas and principles. But he was beginning also to see Oda in a different light. A note in his diary says, 'Do not think of…in this way. If it is my will it will happen. Am I not enough?' 'Yes, Lord.'

While in Holland there are diary entries made at 2 a.m. and 4 a.m. and notes of many people to see and help. Back in England too there were many things going on. In particular, Mahatma Gandhi was visiting England. He had arrived on September 12th to represent the Indian National Congress at the Round Table Conference called by the British government with the aim of working out a new constitution for India—'the substance of independence'. 'I must go to London with God as my guide,' Gandhi had said. Already Murray had met Gandhi in London on September 16th—a meeting arranged by Gandhi's close friend the Reverend C. F. Andrews, a missionary who had worked for many years in India and who had become a dedicated fighter for Indian rights. Clearly, like his brother, Murray longed for Gandhi's conversion, and we can be sure that when he and Gandhi met they will have spoken of the claims of Christ. However, though he admired Jesus' teaching, Gandhi was a Hindu to the depth of his being, and such he remained. Murray went on praying and hoping, and on October 9th he noted in his prayer diary, 'A vision of the baptism of Gandhi in Oxford in December'—something that we know did not take place.

While he was in England in 1931, not only was Murray busy speaking about and recruiting for Dohnavur, but he was also still deeply involved with Frank Buchman's 'Groups'. Although the movement had grown considerably since he left England, the tide of feeling among evangelical Christians was turning against it, and this led to a time of great stress for Murray. Jotted down in his diary are some of the criticisms that were being raised. They seem to be comments made by Christian people who had been to Group meetings and found them unhelpful or even doctrinally adrift:

> "No prayer."
> "Not one verse of Scripture referred to in two hours' meeting."
> "Sharing sins and 'getting release' mentioned six times—nothing to give an idea of the reality of sin."
> "No mention of Christ's work."
> "No mention of the poorer classes at all—no interest in them."
> "Public confession of sins not helpful or right."

Clearly, the criticisms were serious ones. Murray had an evening with Frank Buchman at Brown's Hotel, and commented, 'He and I had a long chat at dinner, alone, and I put up to him all the questions and criticisms of which one has been hearing so much. He answered them absolutely satisfactorily and I felt that Buchman himself was still absolutely sound; he is going deeper and further than six years ago.' On the other hand, writing some years later of this period to a friend who was anxious about his links with the Oxford Group, he wrote, 'I hoped up to the end of my leave that it would be possible to do something to keep the Groups on the lines that I had seen when the few friends I knew were working together in 1920; but it was too big and out of control by then.'

Murray was always utterly loyal; this was part of his nature and part of his creed. The problem now was that conflicting loyalties were tearing him apart. On the one hand, Frank Buchman had helped to transform his Christian experience at a vital stage; on the other, he was beginning to recognize some validity in the criticisms being expressed throughout the evangelical world and to detect subtle changes in the Groups since last he was in England. All this was deeply worrying and must have contributed to his headaches and insomnia.

Meanwhile, there was a sudden setback to the work in India. In November, news reached Murray that Amma had had an accident. On October 24th she had gone some 4 miles to the town of Kalakkadu where a small house had recently become available for use by the Fellowship. In the twilight she had slipped into a pit recently dug there and had dislocated and fractured her left ankle. She was taken at once to Neyyoor where the broken bone was efficiently set by Howard Somervell but, lacking the help of modern physiotherapy, complications had set in. Although no one could have foreseen it at the time, Amma, at the age of sixty-three, was to be largely bedridden for the rest of her life, and things in Dohnavur would never be quite the same again.

In January Murray went to Switzerland for a skiing holiday. He had written to Mr Alexander, the principal of Le Roc Bible school whose children he had rescued six years earlier, asking if he could recommend a skiing companion. Mr Alexander suggested Philippe Berthoud, a young Swiss student at Le Roc who was hoping to go as a missionary to South America. He and Murray stayed at Samedan, a small town near St Moritz.

Philippe has recalled:

We did several trips on skis and there is one occasion I will never forget. It was sunny and we were resting on our skis absolutely alone and talking of the extraordinary beauty of God's creation. Then Murray asked me what I was going to do on my return to Geneva. Well, waiting for a door to open to South America. That was obvious. Then Murray simply said this: "I have no right at all to tell you what is God's will for you. But can I suggest something: if a door is shut and has been shut for so long in front of you, may it not be that another door is opening in a direction where you have not thought to look?"

Of course Murray had often spoken to me about Dohnavur and the need for a practical man to help with the building of a hospital. So I understood exactly what he meant, and for four days I was torn between these two thoughts. To go to Dohnavur would correspond exactly to what I would like most: to use my practical training on the mission field. On the other hand I was "sure" that my call was for South America! Gradually after those four days of struggle it was confirmed to me that God wanted me to go to Dohnavur.

And so Philippe arrived at Dohnavur a year later as the first of many Swiss members of the family, showing once again how God often seemed able to work through a series of events in Murray's life—one act of obedience, or being in the right place at the right time, opening up an area within which the wind of the Holy Spirit was free to blow and achieve his purposes.

All through his European furlough, although under many pressures and often exhausted, Murray was in a state of spiritual exaltation. Walking close to God, he was used wherever he went to draw others closer too. Like the Catherine wheel flaring and sparkling, his brain seemingly unable to rest, he wrote several poems. One was written at Wengen in January 1932 and, set to music later by Godfrey, was to become a favourite children's song at Dohnavur:

Thy happy mountaineer

Make me to be thy happy mountaineer,
    My God most high.
My climbing soul would welcome the austere:
    Oh crucify

On rock, ice cliff, or treacherous field of snow,
    The softness that would sink to things below.

Thou art my guide, where thy sure feet have trod
    Shall mine be set;
Thy lightest word, my law of life; O God,
    Lest I forget,
And slip and fall, teach me to do thy will;
    Thy mountaineer, upon thy holy hill.

At about this time Murray also wrote the poem quoted in Norman Grubb's foreword to this book, 'Make us gay troubadours of God...' It is to this poem that Bishop Houghton referred when he wrote of Murray and his brother Godfrey in his biography of Amy Carmichael: 'The beauty of the Lord our God rested on these two men. They were different in temperament: Murray the more eager, full of initiative, the "gay troubadour of God" that he desired to be, and Godfrey quieter, steady as a rock, perhaps more conservative but no less intense. Both were aflame with the love of Christ, both were walking humbly with God.'[1]

In connection with this poem too, the following incident, occurring years later and recounted by Murray's godson, Dr Christopher Metcalfe, shows how quick-witted Murray was, even in old age: 'I was once telling him on the telephone how much I liked his verse, "Make us gay troubadours of God..." "Did I write that?" he asked. "Yes," I said. "Better change the *gay* to *glad*!"'

A third poem uses yet other images to describe the Christian as Murray saw him (*Gold Cord*, p.272):

    Blasted rock and broken stone,
    Ordinary earth,
    Rolled and rammed and trampled on,
    Forgotten, nothing worth,
    And blamed, but used day after day—
    The open road, the King's highway.

    Often left outside the door,
    Sometimes in the rain,
    Always lying on the floor
    And made for mud and stain;

Men wipe their feet and tread it flat
And beat it clean—the Master's mat.

Thou wast broken, left alone,
Thou was blamed and worse,
Thou wast scourged and spat upon,
Thou didst become my curse—
Lord Jesus, as I think of that
I pray, make me thy road, thy mat.

This last poem reflects some of the stress that Murray was
under, and the sense of being misunderstood. He sent a copy
to Edith Hope-Gill, now at Dohnavur, with this comment:
'These lines came on Christmas day just after leaving
England, and helped.'

Leaving Switzerland, Murray met up with Hugh Evan
Hopkins who was due to travel to India with him. They
sailed out on the *Moreton Bay*. Hugh Evan Hopkins described
the trip:

> To save missionary funds, we went third class in a six-berth
> cabin in the bottom of the ship. It was shared by some Australian
> diggers, one of whom never changed his clothes or socks through-
> out the three weeks it took us to reach Colombo. We slept on deck
> whenever possible! It was a great experience being with Murray
> on board, wandering around, a couple of bachelors, and seeing
> how he got alongside people. He didn't relax or rest, but used
> every moment of the voyage, talking about the Lord, seeking out
> drunks and putting them to bed; we did quite a bit of that. We
> had some wonderful talks with people; watching and listening to
> Murray was an inspiration and I too had the joy of leading some
> to Christ, inspired by the way he went about it. He so really
> cared.

They arrived at Dohnavur in February, as Godfrey described
in the *Dohnavur Letter:* 'February 25th was a day to which the
Family had long looked forward, when Murray and Hugh
arrived, and we sang "O God of Stars" and "Swords drawn"
in the House of Prayer, as we praised God together for his
goodness and pledged ourselves anew to the fight under his
great leadership.'

The children's faces were bright with joyful welcome; the

tubular bells rang out. Amma, chairbound, gave them a loving greeting. Soon the hush of evening fell; the stars of which they had sung shone out in the velvety sky. And in his diary Murray wrote this: 'Praise inexpressible for such a home to come to and for such a homecoming.'

10 Down Under: India, 1932–33, Australia, 1933–35

Ironically, this joyful return marked the beginning of what was, in some respects, a 'low' year for Murray; at times it seemed that the Catherine wheel had almost burnt itself out. Amma wrote in the *Dohnavur Letter* of April 1932: 'The golden joy of the months was the day of Murray's home-coming, bringing Hugh Evan Hopkins with him....But many who know how Murray poured out his strength during the months he was at home, will want to know how he was when he arrived—the answer is, tired, far too tired. It is a costly thing to be an Epaphroditus.'[1] Similarly, May Powell recalled, 'When he returned from furlough bringing Hugh Evan Hopkins, I was shocked, as he drove him round the different parts of our large compound, to see an unsmiling Murray instead of his usual beaming smile.' The stress he had been under during his furlough had marked him and this was evident to his friends.

Hugh Evan Hopkins can remember his first impressions of Dohnavur. He was put with Godfrey and John Risk in the boys' compound. Godfrey he found to be completely the opposite to Murray in every respect—a shade remote, spiritually very intense. Indeed Hugh sensed at once the high level of spiritual intensity throughout the whole Fellowship:

You sometimes felt guilty about laughing, even. The atmosphere was rather like that of a convent. The first morning after my

126

arrival I came down for chota [early breakfast] at 5.30 a.m.
Godfrey and John were both sitting there, so solemn that I
couldn't resist clowning a bit: I put some egg-shell in my mouth
and spat it out vigorously. I'm not sure how amused Godfrey
was, but things did relax a bit after that.

It was marvellous to see it all coming to life—the Fellowship
that I had heard and read and prayed so much about. One had to
realize that under God there was only one boss and that was
Amma. She wouldn't proceed with any course of action until
everyone had agreed, but who dared oppose her? We were
awed—perhaps excessively so—by her wisdom and experience.
She was a remarkable woman, alarming to a raw recruit, with a
sort of aura around her. You sensed at once that she walked very
close to God. Quite apart from her spirituality she was a highly
gifted person—she was very widely read and had an amazing
knowledge of Tamil and of Indian ways. Mercifully she had a
sense of humour, which saved the day many a time. When I first
met her she was not completely bed-ridden but was sitting up in
a chair, already in the famous room from which she hardly ever
emerged.

Indeed Amma, four months after her accident, was not
recovering as well as had been hoped. She was looked after
by Mary Mills, 'the perfect nurse', and, worn out rather like
Florence Nightingale after the Crimea, directed the Fellowship for the rest of her life largely from her bed.

From his diary one gets the impression that Murray went
straight back into his evangelistic, pastoral and medical
work at Dohnavur. There are fewer references to headaches
than in the previous year in England; several references to
the need to talk less at meals, to give others more chance, not
to do jobs that others could do perfectly well, and so on.

While Murray was away, the Fellowship had been encouraged by the baptism of several relations of 'the man mauled
by a tiger', who had been treated in the Door of Health back
in 1928. Now, a few days after Murray and Hugh's arrival,
there was further encouragement and great joy in the baptism
of Silavudeen, the Muslim from Eruvadi who had called on
Murray in Colombo. Godfrey wrote:

On the evening of March 1st we met in the House of Prayer.
There was no mistake about the clear answers which they gave to

the questions put to them. And then we all streamed out in a river of colour to the Red Lake. One by one they went down into the water, Silavudeen the first of his community to confess Christ publicly in these parts, his wife and Devakali ("God's Joy") the first from his village of robber-caste people. After the baptism we rejoiced with the angels and sang psalm after psalm as the evening star shone above the cloud bank, and the shadows spread over the lake.

Such baptisms were moments of glory, but Amma dreaded them too. From long experience she knew that each one aroused the fury of the 'adversary, the devil' and that opposition—either direct, in the administering of poison by an angry relative of the new convert, or indirect, in some illness or adversity striking the Fellowship—would surely follow. Certainly this year was to have its share of adversity.

Building work on the new hospital began again. Philip England, the engineer, had joined the Fellowship at the end of 1931 and had taken over much of the design work and organizing of builders. Norman Burns had also arrived from Australia, and as well as working among the boys was for many years to develop the farm and agricultural work.

Oda van Boetzelaer too had been at Dohnavur since December and was occupied with learning Tamil. She had a remarkable gift for languages, already speaking fluent English, German and French, as well as her native Dutch. Murray saw her all too rarely. He was working in the Door of Health and among the men; she was concentrating on learning Tamil and was sometimes sent to stay in a nearby village or to the Forest for this purpose. In addition, one of the Indian conventions that the Fellowship strove to follow was that, as Murray put it, 'You don't speak to a woman unless she's your wife. When we did meet, we always had to have a chaperone, and we chose the blindest and deafest old lady in our family and parked her at the end of a long verandah!' By this time, Murray was certainly starting to feel admiration and love for Oda, and the hope that eventually she might become his wife. She was intelligent and this was important to him; she was also strikingly beautiful in her Indian sari, with her dark hair, fine features and reserved manner, and she was clearly as eager to serve the Lord here as he was. In addition, Murray was beginning to feel a deep need for someone to stand by and with him, for things were far from well with him.

It is hard to be sure just what the trouble was, and there may have been several contributory factors. For one thing there was exhaustion, already very real, but becoming more crippling with the return to the tropics. This was made worse by his personality: eager, extrovert, anxious to do and to give for his Lord, he was unable to slow down. The exhaustion increased, and with it came feelings of guilt—he should not be feeling like this; he should be doing better and achieving more.

Also, there was the stress of conflict, both external and internal, in connection with the Oxford Group—conflict that began while Murray was in England. Back at Dohnavur it was intensified because of the anxiety that both Amma and Godfrey were beginning to show with regard to Murray's links with Buchmanism. Back in 1925, after Buchman (who admired Amma's work greatly) had visited her in Dohnavur, Amma had written in the *Dohnavur Letter*, 'Let no one judge this man by anything written about him. Frank Buchman is out for one thing only, to win men for Jesus Christ.' Six years later, however, she was beginning to fear that Murray's links with the suspect movement might alienate those Christians with whom the Dohnavur family had most in common. Amma and Godfrey, the two people, apart from his mother and now Oda, whom Murray loved and respected most, were now openly against Frank Buchman, to whom he owed so much. The pain of this conflict was very great. (It was resolved eventually, when Murray circulated a signed statement, dissociating Dohnavur from the Oxford Group.)

Thirdly, although this was not recognized until later, an obscure physical illness seems also to have affected Murray at this time. Some notes from Amma reflected her anxiety:

> Don't be too hard on yourself. It doesn't help. I know there is a weakening softness that is deadly, but that is not the trouble. This weary state of yours does take it out of you. It is all joy, for it is all for God, but the joy has a way of disappearing if on top of everything there is self-blame. So be patient with your tired self—it's part of the daily dying, little as it looks like it.

And in another note, 'Dear dear Murray, I also know the loneliness. I do not think it will be for always, but while it is appointed it can seem very long.'

It soon became clear that Murray had to get away for a while to rest, and at the end of July he went up to the Forest house, and Hugh Evan Hopkins was also sent up to keep him company. Looking back over fifty years or so, Hugh has described their stay. He was young and inexperienced—a good ten years younger than Murray—and clearly mystified:

> I had been seeing very little of Murray—he was working in the hospital and I was with the boys and Godfrey. Then we were all asked to pray for him—he wasn't well. Suddenly I was told to go up to the Forest for a month with him. It was a very strange time. I had no experience of depressive illness, which I now think he was suffering from. I didn't know what was wrong with the man—he seemed to have permanent headaches. I thought it was this Oxford Group business which had got on his mind. We had the forest to ourselves. We just went round like a couple of lumberjacks, cutting down trees, looking for monkeys, swimming. I didn't know what to do with him. He had nothing to say—most unusual for Murray. He used to read a bit, but couldn't concentrate. He wasn't happy—just trying to be happy. It was a strange sort of forgotten month out of one's life. Looking back it seems to me that he was suffering from severe depressive disturbance caused by a combination of exhaustion, driving himself too hard, and the conflict in his mind over the Oxford Group. I don't think he had the theological insight to see that the movement was drifting from the central truths of the Christian faith; he thought of it still as he had experienced it, and as he had put his own truth and knowledge into it. Not being accepted by Amma and Godfrey—this conflict must have caused depression, I would think.

After this break, Murray took up his work again at Dohnavur. At the end of the year, in spite of the difficulties in meeting, he had asked Oda to marry him. He recalled how his own growing love for her was confirmed by the words 'God has given' occurring several times in his daily Bible readings, while to Oda came the more specific words from Psalm 45:10 'Hearken, O daughter…forget also thine own people, and thy father's house.' It is interesting to note that it appears from his diary that Murray had bought a diamond ring before he left England!

Alas, his new happiness did not bring an end to Murray's troubles. In the spring he became seriously ill. He recorded that the illness was meningitis, although Amma referred to it as sun fever. She wrote this hasty note:

> Oda darling,
> 1. Murray must not leave his present room till medical orders (!)
> 2. As soon as he is fit he will be going to the Forest. May Powell takes over for April and May—we will see that she goes away later.
> 3. Oda darling, your times with Murray will do him more good than any other thing but the love of his Lord.

He was seriously ill for six weeks. Then Amma's plan for convalescence in the Forest had to be changed. It was decided that Murray must leave India for a while and go to a cool climate. In England it would soon be summer, and anyway Murray would find no rest there. In Australia winter was coming. Thus it was decided that he should go to Australia for six months, and Amma decided that the best way to facilitate his recovery was for him and Oda to marry at once and go together.

They were married by Hugh Evan Hopkins on 23rd April 1933. Happily Amma was able to be there, and has left this description:

> I wonder if ever a wedding was more simply accomplished. Godfrey held the assembled children singing in the House of Prayer, till Murray, Oda and I came in. And then we all sang, "O splendour of God's will", a Forest song which Murray and Oda had chosen. After this our Tamil pastor prayed and Hugh asked the solemn questions and read the great words, Murray and Oda following in clear voices so that all the children heard; and then came the second song of their choice—"Love through me, Love of God", sung kneeling. It was all solemn and sweet beyond words, and *real*. While the papers were being signed afterwards the children's voices rang in Tamil psalms. A few minutes later the two were gone. But was ever a more soldier-like going?'

Amma goes on to describe how they were taking a sick child
with them to the village where they were to stay until their
passports were ready.

> So as soldiers on service they left us, and I think the Lord must
> have loved their going out and blessed it.
>
> But I have not shown anything properly to you. I see, as I look
> back on those minutes, a packed mass of colour, gay as a garden
> (the children on the floor of the House of Prayer); Hugh standing
> on the blue Persian carpet (but when he is doing his master's
> work one does not see Hugh much, he is more like a clear pane of
> glass than a person), and in the quiet light of the Unseen Presence
> standing very still in reverence are Murray and Oda, he in his
> Indian white, she in her mauve sari, a single rose in her dark hair.
> And now Murray has the *tali*-chain in his hand (the *tali* is the
> Indian marriage token; it is hung on a golden chain—Oda has
> chosen that it should be made like a Passion-flower), and he has
> put the chain about her neck, and is holding it and saying the
> words that crown her, and Hugh is saying the final solemn words
> of blessing, and the three little children who, Tamil-fashion, are
> with them, are smiling up into the lovely face bent down to them,
> and there is a sense as of shining. And this is all I can tell you, for
> it was so simple that there is not much to tell.[2]

They left for Australia at the beginning of May and stayed
first in and around Melbourne, where Murray had periodic
visits to the hospital for treatment. The cooler climate seemed
to help him; he slept better and his headaches began to ease
off. Oda wrote to Amma of the joy of having Murray to
herself—a blessed bonus indeed, for at Dohnavur the pressure
of the community life left married couples very little privacy.
They were happy in Australia, and made many friends.
Murray was having to resist the temptation to start accepting
invitations to speak at meetings; he played golf and benefited
from the fresh air. Financially things were difficult, but
Murray recalled how 'God provided for our needs. One week
we didn't know where the next week's rent was coming from.
A letter came from England, sent off six weeks before, from a
friend of my mother's who had never sent us money before
and never did it again: "£50 for your personal needs", and it
arrived dead on time. That's what God does.'

On September 12th, while in hospital, Murray received a letter that Amma had written soon after her talk with him about the overall leadership of the Fellowship, in February 1931. She had not sent it to him then, but had kept it until now. In it she took up again the theme of leadership:

Dear Murray, can I hesitate to ask what I am asking? Even the uttermost? For is it I who ask or call? No, it is another, and he can not ask too much. I do not think we know to the full the wonderful richness and largeness of the opportunity that has been entrusted to us. It was a Government official who said to me, "Dohnavur is reaching out from beyond south India. It has a mission to fulfil out of all proportion to its size." Sometimes I think that our Lord Jesus wanted to find something which he could take and use for his own glory only—something small enough to be nothing. And so it is a wonderful thing, Murray dear, to be Servant of all here.

In September, Murray was seen by another doctor, who seems to have discovered a definite infection; Amma described it as 'one of those obscure germs which work secretly at first, but surely',[3] and elsewhere as a peculiar form of meningitis (we would now recognize it as viral), the cure of which would delay Murray's return.[4] She wrote to him on October 2nd, 'the relief of knowing that it is a definite infection— something organic which can be fought and conquered—is very great. So it was *this* you had, dear Murray, on your way home, and which you called flu?' If this was correct, Murray had contracted the disease in the summer of 1931, at the start of his furlough. Could this be the sole explanation of his headaches and sleeplessness, or was Hugh Evan Hopkins correct in surmising a depressive illness? We shall never know for certain; possibly a mixture of factors was involved.

Some letters that Evelyn wrote to Murray the following summer (1934), when he and Oda were still in Australia, are illuminating, and show that she understood her son. 'I can rejoice in knowing how beautifully you are taken care of, and loved and understood and valued. It is *such* a rest and comfort to me, for you *are very* precious. The Lord made Oda for you, and I have never met anyone else that would be fitted in so many ways for you.' And again:

I wish when you get back you could go at a slower pace. Do let Oda regulate your pace, and the day's work. She would never want you to be slack, but she is so sane and sensible in these matters—a tremendous gift to you, for it will be very difficult for you to get and *keep* a calm balanced steady pace. Let her teach you how to do this, and keep you calm and quiet. Godfrey can do this more naturally, but you have inherited from me something that tends to speed that is not good, and God has given you Oda to correct this. You are *such* a darling, and always wanting to help and do things for everyone, till there is somewhat of stress at times, and a bit of a rush, perhaps. It may be that to you it will be given to set a steadier pace at Dohnavur. Soldiers on a long drawn-out campaign can do better work when fit than when worn out from want of sleep.

Again, Evelyn wrote for Murray's thirty-eighth birthday, 'Father had a notice up in his room at Cambridge once, "Wanted—more Calebs". How he must rejoice to know that you are seeking like Caleb to follow the Lord wholly.'[5] She wrote quite a bit about homeopathy too, of which she was clearly a devotee, urging Murray to try homeopathic remedies both for himself and for his patients. Murray, though, was not impressed; indeed he tried them once and reported that they made him worse!

Amma wrote regularly too, and so did Godfrey. It was hard for everybody as Murray's return was delayed time and again, but they persisted in trusting God through it all, in the certainty that they were being trusted to cope with the repeated disappointments. In December 1933 Amma wrote, referring to past difficulties and anxieties about the Dohnavur family:

I remember well when that anxiety was heavy on me and I felt if only you and Godfrey were here it did not matter what became of me, and I told the Lord so. He has taken me at my word. He always does I think, and I feel now as I felt then—nothing matters if I have you two beloveds for the leadership of this far-more-to-me-than-my-life Dohnavur. As I see the future it is you, Murray dear, as Leader in general (Servant of all is my name for that), Godfrey with the boys and others too, and May with Arulai, Mabel and others as able with the women and children, doing what neither you or Godfrey could do. And with you Oda, mothering all, loving all, not thinking of any as outside the circle of special tender love.

Amma kept Murray and Oda up to date with news from Dohnavur. Thus in March 1934 she wrote, 'Great news! Christian Rogan is, I believe, the long prayed-for doctor.' And in the same letter. 'I hear the Parama Suha Salai is getting on splendidly. I have not seen it for a long time but hope to go soon and see it all.'

While he was in Australia, Murray thought and prayed constantly about the new hospital that was slowly being built in his absence. In her book *Windows*, Amma recorded the coming in 1934 of what she calls the 'Sign of Completion', just as in 1929 they had received £1,000 as the 'Sign of Beginning' of the work. Murray had sent from Australia some 'cheese-paring' plans, as he felt there was not much money available to finish the building, and this had led Amma to wonder about asking God again for £1,000. Lacking certainty she did not in fact do so, but three weeks later a cheque for £1,000 was received, and they joyfully accepted it as the Lord's encouragement to go on and complete the work, well built, 'magnifical' as it had begun.

Other items of news filtered through. Some changes had been effected in the clothing of the family. Up till now all the men had worn the usual white Indian dress, but Amma had had the idea that it would be more practical and distinctive if the men of the Dohnavur family wore colours—blue and, for the hospital staff, purple. She wrote to Murray, 'The people all around accept our colours and understand them when explained, for that sort of thing appeals (purple humble service, blue love and so on), but going further afield white may be better.' Hugh Evan Hopkins, always anxious to reach 'further afield' with the gospel, disliked these eccentric colours, which smacked of a 'separate' community, but Godfrey and Murray loyally went along with them. The fabric for clothing was woven and dyed on the compound— something of which Mahatma Gandhi would certainly have approved.

After a year in Melbourne, Murray and Oda moved to Sydney where they found a small room, and while there

Murray attended some lectures in tropical medicine at the university. Oda became involved in running a girls' crusader class, and she wrote to Amma from Sydney in August 1934 about a Christian house party that she and Murray had led together: 'Murray really stood it very well; he was a bit tired and we do see again that he is not ready for India yet although one can but praise about the change there is. He can talk with people for hours now and does not feel it an effort at all to concentrate. But the weather is cold here and there is still some way to go before he could do the same thing and do it continually in the heat.'

At about this time Oda realized that she was pregnant, and soon she and Murray moved to a little wooden house that they were lent up in the Blue Mountains some 60 miles west of Sydney. Here they stayed during Oda's pregnancy. Murray had two stories that he loved to tell about this time. One was about a gift. One day Murray had been feeling worried about the future of the Indian work:

> I had one of those half-formed thoughts, "Will the Lord always go on supplying its needs?" The next day a girl appeared out of the mountain mist at the verandah door. She had in one hand a large red rose, and in the other an envelope. She said, "Are you Dr Webb-Peploe?" and gave me the envelope. She had reached the garden gate before I had discovered what was in it; it contained a £1 note. So I called, "Who is it from?" "It doesn't matter. Use it as you are guided", and she slipped away.

Murray took the visit as the answer to the half-formed question of the day before.

His second tale of the time in the Blue Mountains ran as follows:

> Our cottage was on the edge of a valley. We looked down 20 miles over lovely eucalyptus forest. It was the end of the dry weather, and rather hot. I was away for the day, and my wife was there with the woman who came to clean once a week. She looked down the valley and saw a wisp of smoke which soon broadened and spread up the valley—it was a forest fire. Think of 20 miles of eucalyptus trees, dry as matches in a match-box, and as inflammable because the leaves are full of oil; the noise was like

an express train. Oda wondered what to do, but the experienced Australian woman said that there was nothing to do but to get out. Oda replied, "But first there is one thing we can do—we must ask God for help", and so they knelt and prayed. Just as they were leaving, the wind changed through 180 degrees and blew the fire back down the valley. When I came back, there was a patch of grass with one eucalyptus tree left near the house; one side of the tree was scorched, the other green. The house was quite untouched. God's miracle here, as so often, was in the timing.

In April 1935 Oda went into the Charlemount private hospital in Sydney and on April 18th gave birth to not one son, but two. Hanmer Godfrey was born at 4.35 p.m, weighing 6 lb 7 oz, and Michael Murray arrived at 5.5 p.m., weighing 5 lb 11 oz. And so, after an exile of over two years, Murray and Oda returned to Dohnavur with the twins.

11 India, 1935–47

Their return launched Murray on a happy and productive spell of work at Dohnavur, which lasted without interruption for the next twelve years. Possibly the golden glow of 1927–31 was never quite recaptured—those wonderful years when anything had seemed possible. Dr May Powell has described how already in those years, while Amma was still active and to be seen here and there everywhere in the compound and in the surrounding villages, 'she was giving all the time and attention she possibly could to grooming Murray for leadership of the Fellowship. Amma and he were kindred spirits. She loved his enthusiastic response to any challenge. And so they discussed together the whole future planning.' But by 1935 Amma was largely confined to her room, and Murray's illness had subdued his gaiety to some degree. May Powell has said, 'I don't know any word but the now banished "gay" to express his attitude to life before his illness.' Indeed, the gay troubadour of God was what he had most wanted to be. Now things were different but, to use words from St Paul, the Fellowship was afflicted but by no means crushed; struck down but not destroyed. Quite the reverse: it was growing, reaching out in all directions; bursting with life and enthusiasm.

Amma in her book, *Windows*, gave a description that gives some idea of all that was going on.[1] She described the first area inside the 'moon arch' from the street, 'The Round', with the cottages where the schoolgirls lived with their 'accals' (Indian 'elder sisters'), the girls' school and the House of Prayer in the centre. She went on to describe the Square, for little boys and girls aged between two and six, with their kindergarten, their special hospital, and the babies' nurseries. Next comes 'the boy's world, with its great shady trees, courtyards, school-rooms, workshops, weaving-shed, dove-cotes, gardens—and, above all, boys; then the farm and its fields; and again the carpenters' and blacksmiths' work-shops, store-room, engine-room, office and our Indian fellow-workers' homes'; and in the distance the tower of the Place of Heavenly Healing—not yet opened.

With Oda and the babies safely settled in a small house half a mile or so away, Murray settled happily back into the work. One matter to which he gave his attention very early was the Dohnavur family's diet. While in Sydney he had attended lectures on diet and nutrition as well as on tropical diseases, and this had led him to give serious thought to the diet at Dohnavur. The principle was, as in everything, to try to live like the Indians, but at the same time to have a balanced diet, 'because otherwise you cracked up and weren't fit to help the people you had come to serve.' One problem was to get the necessary protein, as no meat apart from chicken could be eaten, out of respect for Indian religious scruples, and fish was rarely available. Extra milk, cheese and eggs were introduced into the diet, also Marmite, as well as more fruit and vegetables. Marmite had an extra virtue, quite apart from its own nutritional value. Murray explained: 'Eggs were an important part of our diet. I always felt it was a pity to lose the protein of an egg that was bad, and discovered that if you add enough Marmite to a bad egg, it camouflages the taste—you get the protein all right! I used to collect bad eggs from the others and eat them in this way.'

Hugh Evan Hopkins who was there valued Murray's real-istic and practical approach: 'It was Murray who brought humanity into Dohnavur. Our nourishment hadn't been properly looked after, and he took practical steps to get it put right. He "earthed us"—he rooted us in reality.' Murray may well have brought humanity to Dohnavur. He was helped by his mother, who was also very practical. Her letters to him in

Australia had many references to this question of an adequate diet at Dohnavur: 'If you could institute *cheese* for tea it would be welcomed, and if Marmite were added to chotah, and Bemax in soups or in porridge, you would be nearer the proper amount of vitamin B. Philip's boils, and other people's troubles would be helped.'

Evelyn now had a lovely home of her own, Northernhay, at Kotagiri in the Nilgiri Hills—a large old bungalow with a beautiful garden. She continued to show warm interest in the work at Dohnavur, and to have young workers in need of rest or study to stay with her. Margaret Evan Hopkins recalls, 'She was a dear old thing; not very tall—a pleasant old lady. She was very good to us all, always ready to help. There were beautiful walks up there on the Nilgiri Hills; one gasped at the beauty.' Similarly, Alice Roberts who taught in the girls' school remembers 'many happy holidays spent at Northernhay with "Aruthal Amma". Our talks over the Bible and her prayers were most inspiring. I loved the times with her.'

Murray felt, as Amma did, that as well as having a diet as far as possible like that of the Indians, it was important too to dress like them, although when working in the hospital the European men wore shorts. Kathleen Grant an Australian member of the Fellowship, gives a splendid description of him:

> He was quite unconventional, and I remember how amused we all were when he arrived on his bicycle in purple shorts, purple being the colour of the hospital uniform. In those days we all religiously wore solar topees. I remember Murray and Koruth Annachie going off to evangelize at an Indian Festival, Murray dressed in the hospital uniform—lavender shirt and purple veshti and a lavender turban. However as it was considered unsafe not to wear a topee, Murray cut off the brim of his and draped his turban round the crown. With his height and this large head-dress he was quite spectacular, though I think he had wanted to be inconspicuous!

Work on the new hospital had progressed slowly but surely while Murray had been away. Everything had been thought of. From the men and women's separate outpatients sections near the main entrance, a covered way led past the office and the dispensary to the three-storey central block of the hospital. This consisted of the operating theatre on the ground floor and, above it, the reading room and the prayer room with its tubular bells and breath-taking view of the mountains. As Nancy Robbins, who was a doctor here from 1946, wrote, remembering her first sight of the theatre: 'It seemed a miracle indeed. The equipment, including the shadowless lamp, the adjustable operating table, the rows of shining instruments in glass-fronted cupboards, and the X-ray installation next door, would do credit to any Western hospital of a similar size.'[2] Beside the theatre were the anaesthetic and sterilizing rooms and the labour ward, and beyond that nurses' rooms, laundry and the milk kitchen. As for the wards, Nancy Robbins described them:

> There are three blocks of wards, planned to meet, first and foremost, the tastes of the patients, and afterwards the convenience of the staff. The private wards are like a row of small Indian houses, each having a private bathroom and kitchen opening off the main room. Here whole families may be admitted; and, because they are able to cook for themselves, their caste customs are not greatly deranged by their sojourn in the midst of a Christian community.

So there the hospital stood, ready for use. The opening had been postponed until Murray's return. It was built solidly in brick, with red-tiled roofs whose corners curled upwards after those in the neighbouring state of Travancore (now Kerala), which had been built by Chinese labour. They believed that if a devil alighted on your roof and slid down an eave to trouble you, the roller coaster curl would conveniently project him into next-door's yard! In Dohnavur it was the hope that every corner should point heavenwards. The verandah roofs were supported by granite pillars—all looked solid, built to last, and built to serve. Amma described the atmosphere inside: 'Much thought had been given to that which is so rarely found in an Indian hospital—quietness; so everywhere there is more space than usual.'[3] She described the Bible verses in Tamil and English written frieze-like on the walls, and added, 'The central tower is set in a garden full of flowering trees, so there is "peace on all sides round about".' Philippe Berthoud, who took charge of the wiring, plumbing and fitting the X-ray plant, observed that when he arrived from Switzerland, 'What struck me immediately was the careful planning together with a touch of beauty.'

The dedication of the hospital, so long delayed, took place on November 15th 1936. It was a beautiful rain-washed spring-like evening. Amma was there, and has described the scene:

> The children gathered near the moon-arch. Everywhere there was colour; crimson lanterns hung in a long line from the rafters, and the tower looked as if someone had thrown a necklet of rubies over his head. The service was all thanksgiving and adoration; the last psalm, "Lift up your heads O ye gates; and be ye lift up, ye everlasting doors; and the King of Glory shall come in", rang out with a thrill that some who heard it will never forget. It was a welcome of the Family to the King of Glory to the place that is his own. After this, the procession of children walked down the inner covered way, the girls singing to the joyful noise of cymbals, triangles and tambourines, and the little ones waving their flags. "There was nothing to spoil it", Dr Orr of Neyyoor said.[4]

Dr Robbins has written a vivid account of the day-to-day working of the hospital. European missionary staff were in charge of each department, and were also responsible for training members of the family as nurses, dispensers and technicians. Outpatient days were crowded with men, women and children milling everywhere and sitting on the verandahs and on benches under the trees, and the doctors, nurses and dispensers trying patiently to deal with them all.[5] As well as purely medical work, time was always found for evangelism and Christian teaching, either through the mid-morning service for the patients, or in small informal groups towards the end of the day. Nobody at Dohnavur was allowed to be purely an evangelist, but each person together with his or her practical calling was always prepared as well to speak for Christ. A member of the Fellowship recalled, 'I used to see Murray standing talking to a man in the outpatients. Suddenly he would take off his sandals and pray.'

Staff were all unsalaried, and lived as part of the community to which, under Christ, they gave their lives while they were

there. One could perhaps liken it to an Israeli kibbutz, but
with the difference that Jesus Christ was its centre and its
Lord. Membership involved complete surrender to him, and
this involved self-discipline. Amma's 'soldierly' concept was
crucial, and even family ties were held to be of secondary
importance to the demands of the Dohnavur family. The
overseas workers had to learn to speak and read the local
language with its complicated script and grammar. They
had to be able to eat Indian food, sitting when necessary
lotus-fashion on the floor before a plantain-leaf plate. They
wore, as we have seen, Indian dress and many of them went
barefoot (even for football and hockey with the boys) and
slept on a thin grass mat spread on the cool verandah tiles.
The Indians too, through being in a community and alongside
Westerners, accepted certain limitations on their own way of
life, and had to contend with endless well-meant inquiries
from the patients:'What is your caste? Why don't you wear
jewels? What is your pay? Why aren't you married?'

Here in the Place of Heavenly Healing Amma had seen an
outlet for the service of 'girls and boys trained to do everything
however menial, as India uses the word, for the love of their
Lord Jesus Christ'. Also, because of the Christian upbringing
that they had received, the Indian hospital workers were able
to withstand the temptations that often came to them in the
form of bribery. The patients were aware that in most
hospitals it was rare actually to be given the treatment
prescribed and paid for, without oiling the palms of the staff.
The fact that this was not the case at Dohnavur became
widely known and added greatly to the Christian witness of
the hospital.

The hospital wards were inexpensively constructed of local
burnt brick with shuttered unglazed windows. Hospital beds
were of simple tubular metal frames laced with wide cotton
tapes supporting a reed mat. Aside from their own ailments
and the all-prevailing mosquitoes, the main source of patient
discomfort was bedbugs. They lurked in the rafters by day to
emerge again at twilight to fresh nightly onslaughts. If they
could be prevented from retreating to the rafters, they could
be dealt with with blow-lamps, and so kept under control.
Somewhere locally Murray found the answer to this problem,

and the new wards were all equipped, head-high round the walls and pillars, with an eighteen inch band of highly polished plaster made from crushed shell-lime. It provided a vertical 'skating rink' that, if kept clean, no bedbug could surmount.

After the happiness of 1936, with the dedication of the hospital, 1937 was a difficult year. The Fellowship went through a fraught time that Amma referred to as 'Adria' (see Acts 27:27). Whatever its exact nature, the trial caused great distress, and Amma recorded that 'it was given to our brave and gentle Murray, who had borne the brunt of the storm, to write the words that met us where we were.' The words were in the form of a poem (*Though the Mountains Shake*, p.15):

The unoffended (Lk 7:23)

If, crushed by mysteries of pain,
You fear to face the storm again;
If, disappointed, you have found
Immortal souls cold, hard or bound—
Your loyalty is to follow me,
Who died for all on Calvary's tree;
And blessed is he, blessed is she
Whoever shall not be offended in me.

If I should count on you to share
The grief redeeming love must bear.
And if obedience brings distress,
Misunderstanding, loneliness—
You follow one through shame and loss
Who knew all grief on that lone cross;
And blessed is he, blessed is she
Whoever shall not be offended in me.

There was joy as well as sadness through that year. At Christmas, Murray and Oda had a special joy in the visit of Oda's parents, who now saw their little twin grandsons for the first time, and were able to share briefly in their daughter's home and happiness before the darkness of the Second World War closed down on them in Holland. They were present at the baptism of eighteen girls in the lake, when 'the air was full of colour, and white herons flew across the water'; they also saw the beginning of a new building—a nurses' house—which was later called *Dayala* after Oda's mother, to whom Amma gave the Tamil name 'Dayalie', graciousness.

With unerring insight Amma chose Tamil names for everybody. Oda was *Deva Vara*—God's gift; Murray, *Deva Mitthiran*—God's friend; Godfrey, *Deva samathanam*—God's peace, Hanmer, *Deva Anmai*—God's soldier, and Michael, *Deva Unmai*—God's truth.

The little boys flourished, although they had frequent illnesses that were a constant source of anxiety to Oda; there were many sources of infection in the Indian heat, and no antibiotics to help. The twins were also beginning to talk, and their remarks amused everyone. The following episode pleased Amma:

> Michael often has boils, those afflictions of the East, and has to have hypodermic injections. These he naturally hates though he manfully tries to rise to the 'Don't cry' standard. But quite on his own he went one better, 'Michael laugh!' he said, and laugh he did. He turned to his mother just as his father slipped the hypodermic needle in, and he laughed.

In May 1938 Godfrey left for England on a six months' furlough, which began with a quiet holiday in the Scilly Isles where he relaxed in perfect weather on the windswept sands and explored the rocky shores with their wealth of wildlife: oyster-catcher, gannet, ringed plover, Arctic tern. It was a time, though all too short, in which to unwind spiritually and to draw new strength from God, and it was here that, moved by the sunlit brilliance of the ocean birds, he composed his Atlantic prayer (song no.66, *Wings*, SPCK):

> Lord, make my heart
>   Pure as the gannet's wing,
> That has no part
>   In aught defiling.
> And make my love
>   Deep as the blue, blue sky,
> Steadfast above
>   The small clouds floating by.

This was one of the beautiful things about the Dohnavur
family at this time—the way that poems and music flowed
out of them. Amma herself wrote hundreds of luminously
spiritual songs, drenched in the imagery of her beloved
mountains and forest, the forest streams and flowers. Murray
and Godfrey wrote them too. The music to accompany them
was 'caught', as they put it, by the more musical members of
the family including Godfrey, and their friends, and then
they were sung by the children. One of Godfrey's early songs,
'Far above the singing stream', set to music written long
before by Evelyn's great grandfather César Malan, was
'exported' to British Columbia via the Chefoo school in
China, where Godfrey had taught it to some CIM children.
In Canada it became a sort of theme song in the Inter-
Varsity camps at the coast, and is apparently still used there
and much loved.

From the Scillies Godfrey travelled north to join Hugh
Evan Hopkins camping with some Cambridge students at
Keswick. Here at the Convention he had the opportunity to
speak for five minutes about the work at Dohnavur. He also
had a moving and wholly unforeseen encounter with a young
doctor, Angus Kinnear, who had arrived almost simultaneously from a climbing holiday in the Outer Hebrides. Angus
had long been preparing himself for medical service overseas,
but had delayed the decision, and now, while returning in a
small boat from the remote island of St Kilda, had felt a clear
call from God to offer for the medical work at Dohnavur. He
had hoped at Keswick to talk to Hugh about this, but was
amazed to find Godfrey there as well. Quickly the two of
them found a strong unity of faith and outlook, and very soon
confirmation was received from Dohnavur that this was
indeed God's answer to a prayer of Amma's ten years earlier,
for a doctor to help Murray with his heavy load. And as she
wrote of Angus's call, 'Only one who has watched an ardent
soul in tired flesh going the second mile with everybody, not
only the medical mile but the spiritual mile too, will understand the relief it was when, at last, Murray had a young
colleague who was in sympathy of spirit with him in all the
deepest things.'

The furlough ended, and in November Godfrey and Angus

sailed together down the Mediterranean from Italy to Cyprus
in a ship laden with Jewish refugees escaping to Palestine
from Central Europe. Tired though Godfrey was from much
travelling in England, he wasted no time in getting his new
recruit started on his direct method of learning Tamil, thus
laying a foundation that was to prove invaluable in the
hospital work.

During Godfrey's absence the Dohnavur family had been
able to buy a large area of rice-fields nearby, and Murray
loved to tell one of his special stories about them:

One day Norman Burns, the Australian who supervised
all the agricultural work of the family, cycled out to Kamaneri
to see how the rice was growing. He was met by the overseer
looking very solemn, who told him that the caterpillars were
out—a rare event that only occurred every twenty or thirty
years, and could result in the loss of the entire crop. According
to the old man there were only two possible things to be done.
One was to flood the rice-fields, but the tank was unfortunately dry; the other was to hire local women to walk through
the fields squashing the caterpillars, but they all happened to
be away harvesting in Travancore. Norman decided to get
the family to pray. This they did, and when he went back
later he was told that a big flock of paddy birds had come and
marched through the rice-fields, eating the caterpillars until
the birds were so heavy that they could hardly get airborne!
So the harvest was saved and the children's food supply
assured for the next six months or so.

In January 1939 Murray and Koruth (the Syrian Christian
from Kerala working with the Fellowship) led a month's
Christian witness in the ancient Hindu town of Veeravanallur,
20 miles to the north. Murray had hoped each year to have
several such 'raiding-parties' to different places, but in fact
the increasing demand of the hospital work made this impossible. With the enthusiastic support of the others, therefore,
Koruth and Murray devised an alternative: perhaps the
people would come to them instead. Two years later, in the
last week of December 1940, they held the first of what was to
become a very significant institution, the Tarisana Kootam
or Meetings of Vision—a week of evangelistic meetings at
Dohnavur. The wards were cleared as far as possible, so that

families contacted over the years could be welcomed and accommodated for a few days. There were no incentives such as free meals or travel to attract them, but the private kitchens made it possible for interested non-Christians of all castes and faiths to come and feel at home, and because of the confidence steadily building up, they came gladly. Each year brought more, and it was wonderful to see the Good News Hall filled with Muslims and Hindus, rich and poor, intellectuals and illiterates, Brahmans and untouchables, all sitting side by side hearing the gospel message. Many have remarked that such a situation is unique. At first the preaching was supplied by Dohnavur staff, both Indian and European, but later more widely experienced Tamil evangelists were invited, and the annual event that Murray initiated has prospered right into the 1980s.

September 1939 saw the outbreak of war in Europe. Murray found it surprisingly hard to understand some of his younger colleagues' anxieties as to whether they should volunteer or not, apparently forgetting his own uncertainty before he eventually joined the Gunners in the First World War. Three British men in fact left Dohnavur to join the forces, but missions were asked to keep their hospital services in full operation. This meant that the hospital staff did not volunteer, and also that Erna Struwe, the German nurse, was allowed to stay at Dohnavur instead of being interned elsewhere. Out of consideration for Erna, the British members of the Dohnavur family refrained from discussing the eagerly awaited war news at mealtimes, but Erna has recalled that one day when the news of the bombing of German towns was particularly fearsome, Murray came and read Psalm 121 and prayed with her, explaining that he felt he must do this before she went to dinner and read the newspaper.

The medical work in the hospital went on into the 1940s, expanding and attracting more and more patients. Sometimes untrained assistants had to be called in to help the over-burdened nurses—particularly during the terrifying outbreaks of cholera. Then an isolation ward equipped with suitable tray-like beds was opened to all comers, who arrived in bullock-carts, barely alive, and could often be revived by transfusions. Among more chronic illnesses, cancer of the jaw and of the stomach were common and were always referred to Neyyoor where Howard Somervell had gained immense experience in this disease, associated apparently with the chewing of betel-nut with tobacco and lime. Accident cases too were common, such as falls from the palmyra palms, and there were several tragic instances where a fractured arm or leg had been too tightly bound by the village medicine man, and in order to save a child's life the limb had to be amputated as gangrene had set in. Lepers too came to a special clinic on Saturday mornings, often walking many miles on cruelly ulcerated feet for the very slight benefit of the treatment then available. The hospital became so popular that the staff could barely cope. Eventually, to allow time for surgery, as well as to save the staff from total exhaustion, the numbers of all-day outpatient clinics (often 350 patients served by only two doctors) had to be reduced from five to three. This was something that Murray regretted, but it was the only thing to do.

In the hospital alone, he was doing the work of two or three people, as were they all, with crowded outpatient clinics, surgery and personal evangelism. Within the Fellowship too, he was always conscious of small things needing to be done to help and encourage here one, there another. His diary, like Godfrey's, is full of reminders about small yet essential details, and in particular he was always careful to keep in touch with Amma, and to encourage her with a visit or a note. His Indian friend, Thyaharaj, observed him closely in the context of the hospital over many years, and came to know him very well. Here are some of his observations:

He had a unique method of approaching individuals; to Murray the importance was in the person. He never thought of an individual as lower than himself; to him the poor and the affluent were equally important, although he would be the first to extend due respect and courtesy to the demanding. He loved to have access into people's homes and into their ways of thinking. It was possibly this understanding of people's thinking which gave him his winsome way of dealing with a situation—saying things which needed to be said in such a way that any resentment was disarmed. He wanted to tell everyone he came in contact with about Jesus, but he never exploited his patients' helpless situation or thrust religion at them. Conviction and conversion must be spontaneous, and this he saw clearly.

With his hospital colleagues Murray had no superiority feeling whatever, and once a colleague had accepted a responsibility he would never interfere. Instead, he would spur his staff on with the familiar words, "Splendid, carry on." He had an infectious buoyancy, always cheerful, always cheering the downhearted. Also he was one of the very few English who would stoop low to apologize and say sincerely, "I am sorry. It was my mistake", and then take steps to rectify the error.

Murray was now at the height of his powers, his heart full of praise for the quiet work of God in many lives. Some patients were clearly converted, like Anandam, a strict and dignified Hindu, who met Christ through reading the Bible and talking to Murray in the hospital, and Vinayaham, an earnest seeker after truth, who having travelled widely to Hindu holy places seeking salvation, eventually found eternal life in Christ at Dohnavur. Thyaharaj has spoken of Murray's unfailing humility in dealing with his patients and with his Indian colleagues, and this surely sprang from his sense of indebtedness to God for all he saw taking place through and around the hospital team.

Sometimes the patients themselves reminded Murray of the need for humility, as in the following amusing incident. One hot day he was conducting the women's clinic, as Christian Rogan was on holiday:

A lady of hers, large, comfortable, who takes life at buffalo-pace, came up in care of her mother. I suggested that a little variety in her diet of polished rice would help, and advised her to try wheat for a change.

"Impossible", said her mother. "She will have no strength on wheat-rice."

"Oh yes, she will", I answered. "I have eaten wheat-rice for six years and I am quite strong."

The mother looked me up and down. "You!" she exclaimed in a voice of scorn. "What work do you do? You sit here all day. She has to do the housework. There is no comparison."

In reality, of course, Murray was working extremely hard. So much so that Amma was anxious. In September 1942 she wrote him this note: 'Is life a bit too hard these days? I miss your lovely light-heartedness somehow—your lovely laugh. You are everybody's helper and inspirer. But you burn your candles at both ends, and sometimes I fear things are too much for you.' Certainly Murray was used to inspire and teach, as well as to help. Some talks he gave in 1943 were nicknamed 'Murray's Brand Essence'—strong meat. And in November 1944 he spoke memorably on 'The Wave of God' to the Fellowship: 'When a great wave at Cape Comorin rolls in upon the shore, it fills the hollows and overflows the pools. The tide is rising; the great wave of God is here. Let us open to that sea every pool and hollow in our lives—the hollows of fear, of loss, of disappointment, of shrinking from responsibility.'

Murray's ability to inspire and help arose from his own close walk with God. As Amma put it, 'He passes on what he receives of the heavenly manna. How often a little note or a card comes to one or another of us, and always there is something written there that tells that "amid the cares and impertinences of the world", as old Jeremy Taylor calls them, there is traffic and intercourse with heaven.'[6]

About this time too, an accident took place. Operating on a man with syphilis Murray cut his finger slightly and contracted the disease. As it was diagnosed at once, it was successfully treated, but the two-year course of intravenous injections was unpleasant. 'Syphilis,' he commented, 'is an occupational hazard of surgeons!'

With her parents in Holland and her brother commanding a submarine in the Far East, the war was a time of anxiety for Oda, and Murray observed that the twins had helped her more through that time than they would ever know. They joined in cheerfully with the small boys at Dohnavur, but as they grew a little older the heat of the plains affected them badly and Oda took them to live in a small cottage in the grounds of their grandmother's house, Northernhay. Lovely though it was, life there was primitive, with no electric lighting or running water. On the other hand, their grandmother owned something very special: one of the original model T Fords: 'Granny's Blue'.

The boys attended a PNEU (Parents' National Educational

Union) school which was run by a group of mothers of ex-patriate children stranded, like themselves, by the war. Oda taught modern languages, and one of Howard Somervell's children, Hugh, was a pupil. To reach Kotagiri from Dohnavur involved an exciting train journey of two days and a night. You would see the train coming into the station, and instead of people's heads sticking out of the windows you would see their feet—evidently the most important part to keep cool. The railway stations too were full of life, with people cooking or sleeping as they waited for their train.

Michael can still recall these years:

Our father was not often with us, but he came up when he could. I remember the enormous labour that we expended to beat flat a cricket pitch at the top of the hill just above Northernhay, and how he would get us all playing cricket when he was there. Later we grew out of that school. Then we moved to another place called Lovedale, just outside Ootacamund, in the Nilgiris again. My mother and Hanmer and I lived there in a little cottage and we went to a sort of crammer's. I remember well my mother's love of animals. At Northernhay we had guinea-pigs, and at Lovedale we acquired a cat and a dog as well. When my father was with us we used to go on quite long bike-rides with the dog on a lead. It was always a moot point whether the dog would go in the right direction! And once there was tremendous excitement when we discovered a cave in a cliff behind the cottage. My father made a special rope-ladder and we used to climb up to the cave. There were bits of old pottery on the floor, so it must have been inhabited once. When our father was free we used to have great fun, and he always used to make time to do exciting things with us.

As for Dohnavur, I remember the House of Prayer, very impressive in its simplicity; also the Easter celebration in the garden. My memories are of Easter being a very special day. We would get up before daylight and proceed with lanterns to "God's garden", which was actually the burial ground. [Both Amma and Godfrey are buried there.] There we would almost re-enact the first day of the Resurrection, and when you met another member of the Family you exchanged the traditional greeting, "Christ is risen", to which the response was, "He is risen indeed"; then you both said "Hallelujah" together.

My Uncle Godfrey I don't remember well; he was a respected but slightly remote figure. I do remember Jack Trehane, who once gave Hanmer and me a well-deserved beating for being cheeky to one of the Indian annachies.

Hanmer too will not forget that painful but salutary chastisement. Of his Uncle Godfrey he recalls a fascinating birdwatching expedition with him, and how well he would sing and strum on his old autoharp.

So the boys spent their childhood in the loving family at Dohnavur, and in the hills and in the Forest of southern India. But time does not stand still, and by 1945 change was in the wind. Soon India would cease to be their home.

12   Changes, 1945–53

Murray worked on through the war years. The nearby small town of Tirrukurungudi illustrated well the effect of his faithful and persistent witness in the neighbourhood. Ever since the days of Jesuit missionary enterprise in the seventeenth century, no Christian group in the south had ever worked closely among the Brahman community, who were the priestly class in Hinduism. One of Murray's ambitions was to break down the barriers of their reserve by talking to them in their homes and learning something of their ways of thinking. Tirrukurungudi, dominated by its Vaishnava temple, afforded an ideal opportunity for this, and soon, to Murray's delight, he was treating some of its people as outpatients, getting to know them personally and slowly winning their confidence. Because of his own personal charm, he could speak to them of Jesus Christ and often get a quiet, respectful hearing. Then, in the early 1940s, Vengadam, son of the *jeer-swami* or high priest of the shrine, contracted typhoid. He was very ill, but there was prayer for him and his family, and after prolonged nursing care in the hospital he survived to return home. From that day the community overcame their inhibitions and became regular attenders at the hospital, and their secluded homes became open to the staff as welcome guests.

Once in 1946 Murray was even invited to visit the *jeer-swami* himself in the sacred precinct within whose walls he

was confined for life. The lonely old man displayed the
treasures and sacred tools of his office and allowed himself to
be photographed. It was a parting glimpse of a closed world
for which Murray had so long prayed and which he was
never to revisit. Years later Vengadam himself assumed his
father's throne as high priest and was confined within those
same high walls, permanently separated from the gentle wife
whom he had loved and who had borne his children. She died
not long after, affirming her trust in the Lord Jesus Christ.
He had meanwhile sent out a message asking for his Tamil
Bible, one that Murray had given him on his recovery from
typhoid.

The photographing of the old *jeer-swami* reminds us that
photography was one of Murray's hobbies. He took many
splendid pictures of the mountains, of the local people, and of
the small children of the family; several of his photos were used
as illustrations to Amma's books. His other hobby was
mountaineering, and there was great scope for taking parties
of boys climbing in the massive granite-cliffed mountains to
the west of Dohnavur. Once, with Howard Somervell, he
took a party of Dohnavur boys climbing Tiruvannamalai,
the 4,600-foot peak that towers almost vertically above the
plains. This was to be his last memorable climb in the
southern hills, for now that Murray was nearly fifty unexpected changes were to wrench him, much earlier than could
have been anticipated, from the Dohnavur family and from
the work he loved. Murray's life and that of the family were
profoundly affected; neither would ever be the same again.

The first hint of change can be found in Oda's diary, where
she wrote on April 7th 1945: 'Feeling it impossible to sacrifice
H. and M., rather leave D.F. Asked for special word. 1
Samuel 1 and 2 given.' As early as December 1944 Amma
had written a note to Murray that seems to show that the
pressures of life at Dohnavur and her anxieties about the
boys' frequent illnesses were already getting Oda down.
Amma had written, 'A tired (ill) body, an overstrained mind
are not responsible for feelings.... The real Oda has twice
shone through the mists the cruel enemy has flung around
her.'

Hanmer and Michael had almost reached their tenth

birthday. Because of the war they had been longer in India than most European boys. Howard Somervell, writing in his book, *After Everest*,[1] says emphatically that 'a boy over six should not stay in the East, for the climate is so hot and soft that he gets no resistance to chills and chest diseases. He is also apt to have his head turned by thinking he is a "little Sahib".' At any rate, with the war ended, the time had clearly come when Hanmer and Michael should start schooling in England. Oda felt she could not send them off on their own and continue with her work at Dohnavur; she must go too, and make a home for them.

Arrangements were made for them to start at a boarding preparatory school in the north of England, and the three of them set off. The boys started school in the autumn of 1945. Oda had no settled home, Bracken Glen having been sold in 1941, but she found herself a job teaching in a girl's school in Dorset. Things were far from easy. England was a foreign country to her; she was not at home with English ways. She had no relations of her own there, although Murray had made her a list of his relations and friends with whom she no doubt got in touch. Her life at the school was not happy—she was overworked and underpaid. In the holidays she and the boys lived out of suitcases in different people's homes, or else at the Dorset school. They did not go back to Dohnavur for the holidays, presumably because of the expense. They went to Holland though, to Oda's family, in the summer of 1946— a wonderful reunion after the anxiety and horror of the war.

Murray wrote them loving letters. Sometimes he had to write sternly to the boys. It seems that when Oda visited them at the school she had found their manners not up to scratch. Murray wrote to them sadly, 'This simply will not do. You know that I hate having to write and strafe you; it is up to you to pull up.' Similarly, he was worried about their friendships: 'What are these friends of yours really like? Do they tend to make you fool when you should be working? Do they help you to follow the Lord Jesus? It is quite right to be nice to everybody, but you must be careful whom you choose for your close friends.' Another time his letter consisted of a lyrical poem, which, as he told them, came to him during a sleepless night after some injections he had to have at

Dohnavur:

'Do you still remember?'…A South Indian forest holiday

(To sons in England)

Do you still remember the magic, moonlit hour before the dawn,
    The bumpy bandy journey, and the Lotus Lake's clear calm,
Where Tiruvannan towers, like a giant washed and shorn,
    And early bamboo cutters stop to stare and say salaam?

Do you still remember the trek, across the bouldered torrent beds,
    By twisty cattle paths amid the thorn scrub and the sand,
While sentries of the foothills lift their bushy, rock-crowned heads
    And carefree birds are singing, 'Hallelujah, life is grand'?

Do you still remember the Forest boundary, cairns of hoary stones,
    And open grassy slopes, a haunt of tiger and of deer;
The little streams—by one lie yet the long-dead Sambur's bones—
    And Naval trees, beloved of bears, that all the coolies fear?

Do you still remember Rest River, and its whispering bridge,
        and then
    The shady halt, the opened pack, the memorable drink,
And all the happy chatter of the friendly garden men
    Who leave their loads, and eat their rice down by the
        river's brink?

Do you still remember the long, slow, sun-baked, upward-winding
        track,
    The steps of Kashtagiri, which the coolie-carriers hate,
And at the top the pause to get your breath, the far view back—
    The patchwork plain, the silver sea, Heaven's wide-flung
        morning gate?

Do you still remember—I showed you both—the dim-lit, level
        length
    Of jungle, where I saw a full-grown tiger cub so near;
(I can see now his golden glory and his massive strength).
    I stood; he passed in silence, as cloud-shadows disappear.

Do you still remember the beauty of the Upper River pool;
    The last, steep zigzag climb; the harsh cicada's cry;
The royal carpet of red leaves, the fairy ferns; the cool
    Fresh mountain wind; the weathered roof against an azure sky?

Do you still remember our Forest house, a jewel set in green,
  The welcome of the others, the countless cups of tea;
The Monkey Bridge, the monkeys; gentle sounds of things unseen;
  The Whistling Schoolboy's liquid notes; the great wild-mango
    tree?

Do you still remember our Father's gift—that crowning joy of all—
  The Marahatha [emerald] Pool; the cheerful song, the
    clean-limbed dive,
The waterfall, the little fish that bite your toes, the call
  Of friend to merry friend?—Yes, it is good to be alive!

But by now serious trouble was beginning to brew, which
profoundly affected Murray and which was to strike at the
root of all Amma's hopes and dreams. Oda was finding life
unbearable in England on her own. Without their father the
boys still did not seem to be developing as she had hoped; she
was struggling to make ends meet, alone in an alien culture.
Murray seemed blindly unaware of what she was suffering;
he was wrapped up in his work at Dohnavur. As Murray put
it years later, 'I was blind and wrong. She was right and
bitter. We were drifting apart.' In desperation, Oda went for
help to the Reverend W. H. Aldis, Home Director of the
China Inland Mission, who was then chairman of the Keswick
Convention. Now began a time when, together with much
prayer, an agonizing tug-of-war was fought over Murray.
Letters flew in all directions.

Evelyn, now seventy-two, rallied vigorously round her
daughter-in-law, and against, not Murray, but her old friend
Miss Carmichael. She too wrote to Mr Aldis, asking him to
help: 'You know already the sorrows my dear daughter-in-
law is passing through on account of my son's view of the will
of God for him preventing him returning to England to be
with her and to make a home for their boys, which is breaking
her. I have sought again and again to point out the duty of a
husband and father in God's word.' As Evelyn saw things,
'Miss C. took possession of Murray and dominated him,
although he seems quite unconscious of this fact.' And to
Murray she wrote similarly, 'Years ago you sought my
counsel...but those days passed, and another woman (not
Oda) took that place, though you may not have realized it.

The Lord has given me the victory, so it has not separated us, thank God.'

The action that Mr Aldis took is reported in a letter to Evelyn dated March 2nd 1946: 'I promised Oda that I would think and pray over the matter and that if I felt so led I would write to Murray.' Anxious lest by trying to help he might in fact make matters worse, he wrote a letter that he kept in a drawer for four months. Then, when he felt it was essential, he sent it off, and later reported to Evelyn, 'Since then I have had a cable from Murray gratefully acknowledging the receipt of the letter.'

Murray's response was typical of his humility. As he commented years later, 'Mr Aldis sent me a jolly stiff letter. In my ordinary Bible reading I was reading in Leviticus all about the Jubilee, and in the Jubilee year, the fiftieth year, it said that every man shall return to his family in the fiftieth year [Lev 25:10]. I was fifty that year!' So once again God strengthened his faithful and humble servant by making him certain what he should do. It seems strange that to somebody as deeply loyal as Murray was, for the second time in his life a conflict should arise between two loyalties. The adversary must have known how such conflicts would have torn him apart. It was hard to abandon a call so clearly given and then so strikingly confirmed in its results.

As for Amma, she tried to be brave. Can we blame her if after the spiritual warfare of 1926–28 she felt that Oda must be wrong? To Murray she wrote, shortly before his final decision, 'Murray dearest, are you breaking your heart because you think we won't be with you if you have to do what you never meant to do? Don't feel like that. Whatever you must do we shall be with you in eternal love. Do you remember the golden days of 1928 when you became *sonthum* —days of heaven on earth. Nothing can take those days away from us.' And in March 1947 she was given the grace to write a little note to Oda, occasioned by the news of her brother's safety after the Japanese invasion of the Dutch East Indies where he had been stationed with the Dutch Navy: 'Oda belovedest, you know without words to tell you, how much I rejoice in your brother's safety. Much love, darling—Your Amma.'

Amma did not write often to Murray after he left Dohnavur, partly because of her increasing weakness, but also they seemed to have an agreement that she would not. But she left a letter, written in July 1947, to be given to him when she died. In it she wrote of 'looking forward to the day when we shall meet in Light—all shadows folded up in light'. She said too, 'I am not writing in answer to the little welcome notes that come from time to time. I sent my answers as you asked me to, via heaven. I thank God as I remember the years of splendid comradeship. Blessed, blessed be the giver of those years—and when I see you again, Murray, it will be all joy—the fullness of joy.'

Should so much be revealed about the inner struggles and sufferings within a Christian fellowship? The Bible does not cover up the disagreement between Paul and Barnabas over John Mark (Acts 15:36–41), and it would seem that only as we see something of the depths and darkness that Christians go through in such righteous dilemmas, and only as we see their faithful response in trusting and following the light that God has given; only as we see God's grace appearing in humility, acceptance and forgiveness; only so does full glory go to the Father whom all of them—Amma, Evelyn, Oda, Murray—sought above all to serve. And as Murray commented years later, 'God guides through thought (intuition), through the Bible and through circumstances. Each couple must get their own guidance from the Lord, and he is sovereign as to the outcome.' He was always very definite about this: he and Oda had been guided in a particular way, but for another couple God might have a quite different solution.

Now Murray, having seen clearly that, as he put it, 'it was absolutely clear that I must come home and make a home for my family', acted with his usual energy and determination. He wrote to Oda in September 1946 from Kotagiri: 'My own belovedst, we do need to be together as soon as we can for the next lap of the road. I can see that very clearly; and that is the Father's plan, I am sure.' And while he was packing up: 'Treasure, this clearing up is a sweat. We are at it all day, pretty well...but we are getting on, and it is good to know that everything packed up will be unpacked *with you* in the home that is to be. You precious thing—it will be wonderful to see your dear face again—even under a modern hat!'

The plan was that Murray and his mother would come home in February the following year. Murray had—providentially—been invited to join his old friend Harold Ball in his medical practice in Barton on Sea, Hampshire. The offer came, a house was found and a car was provided. Three miracles within three months. Murray and Evelyn sailed from Bombay in February and reached England in one of its worst winters.

Many loving letters followed them from the Dohnavur family. Clearly many were expecting Murray to return. Thyaharaj in particular found it difficult to go on working in the hospital without Murray. He wrote that 'humanly speaking, the stimulus has gone. But the Lord Jesus Christ is the same yesterday and today, and so it matters very little whether you are in England, or we here, as our Centre is the Lord.' Bravely they carried on, and gradually the team knit itself together again to face the next major change that took place shortly after Murray left—the granting of independence to India.

British rule in India had originated in trade. As James Morris put it, 'the gentlemen of the East India Company had not originally intended to govern India, but merely to make money there.'[2] Gradually their role became more and more one of governing and administering the country. The British Raj was established, but not until the end of the eighteenth century did the Christians in England begin to realize their responsibilities to meet the vast spiritual need of India. After much campaigning, William Wilberforce and others succeeded in 1813 in getting the charter of the Company altered by Act of Parliament to include the need to take responsibility for the 'introduction of useful knowledge and of religious and moral improvement', while maintaining the right to religious freedom of the Indian people. From now on, the door was open for the preaching of the gospel all over India, although particularly in the south it had been introduced centuries earlier, both in the ancient 'Syrian' church, traditionally founded by the apostle Thomas, and by Francis Xavier.

Amy Carmichael had arrived in India in 1896. The church

was then as always particularly strong in the south, but there was too much nominal Christianity based on mass conversions, and that among the lowest castes who had much to gain by becoming Christian. Amma attempted something difficult, often ministering to those for whom turning to Christ meant loss of caste and ostracism.

Following the formation of the Indian National Congress and Gandhi's Civil Disobedience Campaign, it was inevitable that as soon as the war ended, Indian independence would be declared. This was effected by Lord Mountbatten on August 15th 1947. Godfrey wrote:

> The great day 15th passed off quietly. The village had a few fireworks and chorused shouting of 'Victory to India'. We had a very simple talk on the change of government by Thyaharaj, and then we put up the new flag of India and stood around it and prayed for the country. There was no visible difference on August 16th. Rumours were flying, about the English leaving on the 15th and other foolish things, but it is just talk and will soon settle when they see it is not so.

Godfrey had been left with a tremendous burden of extra work when Murray left. The medical team had been greatly strengthened by the arrival of Dr Nancy Robbins in 1946, and a little later Lieutenant-Colonel Ronald Taylor from the now disbanded Indian Medical Service but, as Bishop Houghton observed:

> Murray's departure probably meant more to Godfrey than anyone could understand. They had been a team...Murray's initiative and Godfrey's steadiness were both of immense value, but it was a value which was more than doubled when they worked together. Now it was necessary for Godfrey to take over some of Murray's responsibilities, and the load was too heavy.[3]

As early as February 1946 Godfrey had recognized what would happen. He had written to his mother while Murray was still at Dohnavur:

> I expect Murray has written to you about his new thought. When you pray for me, remember, please, the very greatly added

burdens that it seems as if it must bring to me. I have always tried
to avoid leadership, yet it seems as though more of it will be
thrust upon me. *This, mother dearest, is only for you.* I shall need all
God's grace and fulness to shoulder this, and I count upon your
prayers.

Indeed, all God's grace and fulness were given to Godfrey,
and he shouldered the extra burden with his usual care and
thoroughness. The changed atmosphere and sense of unrest
in India saddened him, and he seemed to have some pre-
monition about what the future held. A few days after independence he wrote this to his mother, 'I am so glad you are
near Murray and so can see him every now and then. I expect
we shall next meet in heaven, and it will be a better meeting
place than this earth, this poor old unpeaceful earth.'

In the summer of 1948 Godfrey's burden was further
increased. Amma, who since independence was needed more
than ever to hold the family together, slipped in her room, fell
heavily and was seriously hurt. For the remaining two and a
half years of her life she was not able to be in any sense the
leader of the Fellowship as she had continued to be since her
first accident.

In January 1949 Godfrey was formally elected as co-leader
of the Fellowship; this meant that he was now authorized to
make important decisions without consulting Amma.
Godfrey, possibly more than Murray, was ideally suited to
take this responsibility at this time. He was loved and respected, and knew everybody in and around Dohnavur. Like
Enoch, as Amma recognized, he walked with God. Also, he
was prepared to consider and rethink policies and long-
established customs. In this flexibility of mind he was superior
to Murray, in whom loyalty sometimes led to inflexibility.
On December 9th he had written to Evelyn saying that he
was very well in spite of so much to do, and telling her that
'the Lord is beginning to move in our midst in a new way—
not perhaps the way we expected, but in the last two days in
talk I have had with a number of Anandas I have seen the
beginning of something we have longed for for years and
never quite knew how to begin to do.'

But by December 27th he wrote, 'Forgive only a wee note.

I am not very fit. Just before Christmas I had a funny leg—some sort of slight stop in the circulation. Then on Christmas afternoon I got an inflammation which has gone on—up and down—cause unknown. I have to lie flat, hence this very "worse than usual" writing.' He had a thrombosis in the leg. In January, when he was elected as co-leader, he was still in bed with his leg immobilized in a splint, but seemed to be making good progress. Towards the end of January his lung appears to have become affected. He wrote home on January 30th, 'Last week I fear that I was rather "blotto" and only managed one line, but this week I am climbing out of the pit. I have so much to be grateful for...'

He wrote again on February 6th, 'I hope that this week will see the beginning of movement for my leg. My head is quite restored to normal, so that I can read books all day without feeling tired.' It seemed that he was well on the way to recovery, but almost without warning he was taken seriously ill again on February 19th, with a coronary thrombosis, and within moments was face to face with his Lord. 'Enoch walked with God. And he was not; for God took him' (Gen 5:24 AV). Godfrey was forty-seven.

How should we begin to assess the impact of his life and death? 'Whenever I see him, he makes me think of the Lord Jesus', one little Indian girl in the family had said, and a member of the Fellowship who wrote to Evelyn after seeing Godfrey's body 'lying so peacefully and yet like a victor, which he is', continued:

> One of his favourite verses came to mind: "Blessed are the pure in heart, for they shall see God'....That is the portion of our beloved Godfrey this very day. On coming down from the Forest he told me in a note that he had received a great spiritual blessing. The added fragrance of his life testified to this. It was that that caught at my heart all through his illness—he seemed so ready for the fuller life.

Amma, as always, responded bravely and trustingly. Commenting in a printed circular letter on the words with which Mary Mills, the 'perfect nurse', had told her of Godfrey's death: 'Nothing is wrong. God has trusted us with a great trust, Godfrey is in heaven', she wrote, 'So from the beginning I think we all took this sudden parting as indeed a great trust, and our prayer all along has been that we should accept it in faith and go on, fearing nothing.' She recalled:

> Godfrey was with me last on his Coming Day, December 15th 1948. There was a sense of stillness about him, and of purity like the purity of our tall white mountain lilies. He had often reminded me of those flowers, so tall, so pure, so fragrant, and on that day it was more so than ever. As he left the room I remember saying to myself, 'Will you walk across the Border before I see you again?'

She wrote of his thoroughness and dedication: 'Many words could not tell what Godfrey was in utter devotion and selflessness. Nothing was too much for him to give or do. There was nothing left undone, nothing forgotten that could help anyone, young or old, inside or outside of this large family.'

She wrote too about his love and knowledge of nature, of:

> his love for birds and flowers and all the beautiful things our Father made for us. He found a new world in our tropical forest, which climbs the mountains near Dohnavur, and he never got to the end of the wonders of that world. He shared his knowledge with the Bombay Natural History Society,[4] and was in touch also with the British Museum and with Kew Gardens. His was not a narrow life.

Finally she wrote about herself:

> I used to say to the Lord, "Lord, if thou dost give these two brothers to be leaders of the Fellowship it does not matter what happens to me. Let me be broken if only they may be strong and fit." They have both gone and I am left quite broken, but content, for I know that we are safe in the hands of the mighty and loving One to whom this Fellowship belongs.

Bravely, in the rest of the letter she looked ahead; spoke of John Risk, Godfrey's 'Joshua' who would now take over leadership, and of the adjustments that would have to be made in leading the family forward under the new Indian government.

As for Godfrey's acquaintances and friends, hundreds of letters were written to Murray and to Evelyn on Godfrey's death. Thus Canon Bob Howard, then Master of St Peter's Hall, Cambridge, wrote, 'I have such vivid recollections of Godfrey as a boy and in his youth. He always seemed so singularly pure, wholesome and happy'; Howard Somervell wrote of having visited Godfrey twice during his illness: 'The boys will so miss him—they not only loved him but did *so* respect him. So did I; yet one never felt that inferiority complex when with him—he himself was always so obviously and sincerely humble.' A member of the Dohnavur family wrote, 'To me his friendship has been the most precious gift God ever gave me'. From England also, Godfrey Buxton and many others wrote of God's foreknowledge and care in that Evelyn was with Murray and Oda when the cable arrived with the news of Godfrey's death. She had moved to live with them ten days before.

Evelyn found it hard to bear this blow. She was getting old. Perhaps she had already realized that, as Godfrey had written, their next meeting would be in heaven, but she could not have expected it would happen this way. In 1947, shortly before she left India, Godfrey had written her a special letter in which he had tried to sum up all that he wanted to say to her:

> My own dearest mother,
>   This is just to write what I cannot ever adequately say of gratitude for all you have meant to me, and for all you have gone without that I might have all the privileges that I have enjoyed …above all, thank you for your wholehearted giving of me to the Lord and to his work. He still, I believe, wants me in his work at Dohnavur. Please pray that I may know the "crucified" life every day, and that I may be faithful to the end. I can never properly thank you for all the way your life and love prepared me for God's call and work; and for all the help you have been through these years in India. "Except a corn of wheat fall into the ground and die, it abideth alone; but if it die, it bringeth forth much fruit." May it be even so for us.

Like some of Evelyn's letters, this one too seems to have a curious prescience. Perhaps it helped to prepare Evelyn for the bigger separation from Godfrey that was to come.

And finally to Murray's feelings. In fact, there is no record

of how Murray felt over Godfrey's death. One can surmise,
though, that he must have been tempted to blame himself, in
that his leaving Dohnavur had placed an extra burden on
Godfrey. But he would have dealt with this temptation in a
realistic and truly Christian way. Like Amma, he would put
on the shield of faith to ward off the fiery darts of the evil one,
and trustingly go on.

There was one more major change to come at Dohnavur.
On 18th January 1951, Amma herself, now eighty-three and
having been at Dohnavur without a break for fifty years,
went peacefully to be with her Lord. She had not lost. She
had gained everything she could have hoped for, and was
content to leave God's work, not hers, in his good hands. She
had seen the growth and flowering of a remarkable community throughout the first half of the twentieth century
when it was able to reach out into the south Indian countryside for Christ in an unprecedented way. With the coming of
independence, the pattern of life and witness of the Fellowship
was bound to change; it was necessary and healthy for Indian
leaders to come to the fore. When at last in 1951, Amma
herself, 'quite broken, but content', went to be with her Lord,
the Fellowship was ready to go forward with God into a new
era of service.

Murray, meanwhile, was adapting himself to a fresh role
with his usual enthusiasm and attack. For the next thirty
years he was to live and work as a much loved GP in the
English New Forest.

13   New Forest GP, 1947–82

The medical practice that Murray's old Weymouth friend, Harold Ball, had invited him to join was in Hampshire, at Barton on Sea. Woodley, Murray and Oda's new home, was a big Edwardian house with a large garden and orchard, on the main road coming into Lymington from the north. It had belonged to an old lady who kept twenty or more cats, and in the process of moving in they found several cat corpses in varying stages of decay in the attics—it took months to get rid of the smell! They bought an adjacent field as well, and Oda's love of animals and the post-war need for home produce soon began to be satisfied as pigs, hens, geese, goats and bees were added to the ménage. The orchard, lovingly tended, supplied them with apples, plums and damsons galore; tomatoes, vegetables, strawberries and raspberries were planted as well.

For a couple of years Murray helped Dr Ball with the Barton practice, but before long he started attracting to it people from Lymington as well. Gradually a second practice grew up there. Until 1948, when the National Health Service was formed, Harold Ball had been doing anaesthetics at Lymington hospital as well as his general practice work. Under the NHS he was not allowed to do both jobs and so handed over the practice to Murray, who for some years ran the Lymington practice himself and had a trainee assistant to run the Barton surgery. Both areas of the practice were

growing fast and it was impossible for one man to run both
ends.

It seems that Murray didn't immediately get the measure
of things in England. Insight into his transition from the
medical missionary to English GP is given by a newly qualified doctor who did a short locum for Murray in his early
days at Lymington. He observed shortly afterwards:

> Murray Webb-Peploe is a remarkable person and is going to
> have a great influence in the neighbourhood. But he has forgotten
> that he is not now in a mission hospital labelled "Christian". He
> talks to everybody, and apparently lengthens the surgeries and
> keeps people waiting while he shares the gospel with his patients.
> But in Britain, if you go to a doctor you expect him to be
> primarily interested in your ailment!

Similarly, we are told that the new locum, trained in all the
latest office methods—filing of case-records and so on—was
a little surprised to find at Lymington what to him was an
elementary system suitable for an Indian village! The young
locum was able to instruct Murray in the demands of the
British law as regards poison records, so that all was in order
before the government inspector came. With the help of a GP
refresher course, Murray quickly learnt and adapted to his
new situation, and his warm personality and care for each
individual, as well as his considerable medical experience,
soon drew many people in the area to his surgery.

Now began a long period of happiness and fruitfulness for
Murray and his family. The boys were much more secure
now that they had a settled home and were reunited with
their father. Indeed Hanmer said later that he was sure he
would have gone steadily downhill if his father had not come
back from India at that time. From their prep school they
transferred in 1948 to Clifton College, Bristol, where they
both made the most of all their opportunities, excelling in
sport and music, developing their lives as active Christians,
and studying hard as well. Michael was becoming certain
that he wanted to be a doctor; Hanmer was less sure as to his
future but was developing an outstanding singing voice.
Both had good friends whom they loved to invite home to
Woodley for the holidays.

Life at Woodley was great fun; they would help their mother with the 'farm' and, even greater joy, go out with their father on *Minx*. *Minx* was a 16-foot Bermuda-rigged sloop, loaned to them by Lieutenant-Colonel Ronald Taylor who had been a doctor for a while at Dohnavur. It was he who looked after Godfrey in his last illness. Hanmer and Michael, helped by the 'postman gardener', Mr Hunt, painted *Minx*; they also overhauled the rigging under the tuition of the other gardener, Mr Gates, who had been mate on a coastal schooner before the Great War. From then onwards, whenever Murray was free and the boys were at home, the three of them would go off together on the river. They all loved sailing; and, as in India, the boys loved doing anything with their father. Always these outings were fun; although sometimes they were frightening. Michael can remember in particular a trip alone with his father when they crossed the Solent to the Isle of Wight and various accidents led to their being in very serious trouble on the journey back. Both confessed afterwards to praying hard. They reached home safely, and the shared danger had forged an extra bond between father and son.

Indeed, the bonds between all four—mother, father and the twins—were strong. And yet, although Murray and Oda always tried to keep some time free when they and Hanmer and Michael could be alone together, Woodley was fundamentally a hospitable place; a home whose members looked not primarily inwards on themselves but first upwards to God and then outwards to other people.

Countless people found rest and refreshment and a welcome at Woodley, the boys' friends among them. Many a talk took place around the kitchen table and above the mantelpiece hung one word on a board: OTHERS. Whatever was going on, the guests would be invited to join in. Anyone staying in the house would be included in the sailing trips—whether they enjoyed sailing or not! Michael can remember 'a high-up Nepalese legal chap who came down for a Whit-weekend and we took him sailing. He couldn't swim so he sat in the bottom of the boat wearing a life-jacket. There was an almost flat calm, but he sat gripping on to each gunwale obviously terrified. Afterwards he confessed to having had "much fear".'

Guests would also be put to work feeding the animals, or in the garden, the more agile ones being useful for climbing trees and picking the fruit. The 'farm' was another area of life and work—and enjoyment—at Woodley. Milk was still rationed, and it seemed prudent to start keeping goats. Oda had adored animals since her childhood, and soon the live-stock became an essential and much-loved part of the family. Michael and Hanmer learnt to milk the goats and to act as midwife when the kids were born.

Once the beloved goat Emmy contracted pneumonia and the vet prescribed whisky. Murray, who normally never darkened the door of a pub, was happy to go round to the local to buy half a bottle of whisky for the benefit of the goat. But it was generally Oda who fussed over all the animals. Murray's partner, Hubert Edmunds, found it strange: 'They had two or three cats in the house. He graciously suffered them provided they kept to the kitchen. They were Oda's pets.' Murray was fond of animals—his concern for the horses during the First World War, and his adoption of 'Jimmy' both show this—but he would not pamper them unduly. His affection showed itself, even with the animals, in practical service. The busy Lymington GP could often be seen stopping on his rounds to cut ash-switches (by arrange-ment!) for his goats to nibble at and, he would reach home with them piled in the back of his car.

Life at Woodley seems to have been a happy mixture of hard work, fun and spirituality. Murray would exercise a characteristic ministry over the washing-up. A guest would be provided with a cloth and, while Murray energetically washed, many a deep and worthwhile conversation took place. Oda too was warmly hospitable; everything was thoughtfully and graciously done to make her guests happy. It was her major ministry, and she too helped many by her friendly listening and her wise advice. The effect on a guest of a stay at Woodley is well summed up in this extract from a letter to Oda from George Bennet, a young teacher at Clifton College who became a friend:

I don't know where to start to thank you for my delightful stay. Surely yours must be the happiest home in England, and you made me feel at home in it at once! I don't think I have ever been in a house where there was such a restful atmosphere in the presence of such ceaseless activity. And what fun it is putting up someone else's chicken-house! I feel more rested and fit than I have felt for a long time.

This letter is an impressive tribute to a family that only six years earlier had been in grave danger of falling apart.

Another area of hospitality consisted of the informal 'think parties' that Murray and Oda began to hold in their home, when friends, neighbours and patients would be invited to hear a talk on some aspect of the Christian faith. Possibly, Murray conceived the idea of these gatherings as a way of sharing his faith with his patients without using up valuable surgery time. At any rate, they were very popular, with sometimes forty or fifty people crammed into the drawing-room, hall and on up the stairs, with the speaker standing in the doorway so that all could hear. Oda dispensed coffee and made everyone feel welcome; Murray opened and closed the meetings with his usual mixture of wit, geniality and serious-ness; and many people still look back on those meetings as the turning point of their lives. One notable speaker was Corrie Ten Boom, whose father and sister died in a Nazi concentration camp for persisting in sheltering Jews in Holland; another was a colourful character, Alf Schultes. He had been born into an ancient aristocratic family in south Germany and on being converted to the Christian faith became a pastor and began running a youth club. He was imprisoned at the start of the Second World War for refusing to allow his club to be incorporated into Hitler's youth movement and later miraculously escaped and came to England, where he ran a smallholding. He became a regular speaker at the Woodley 'think parties', as well as a wise and good friend.

At Lymington too, Murray became involved in another form of evangelistic outreach. Although he was not a member himself, he had a close friend, Major Bill Martineau, also a Christian, who was vice-commodore of the Royal Lymington Yacht Club. Once a year they jointly sent formal invitations to the largely ex-service club members, inviting them to hear speakers who were always carefully chosen to interest them. Oda's brother, Captain Charles Baron van Boetzelaer, spoke there once, no doubt recounting his remarkable escape from the Japanese; on other occasions Sir Frederick Catherwood, Admiral Sir Horace Law, Lieutenant-General Sir John (Pasha) Glubb, Professor Sir Norman Anderson and many others visited—each testifying in different ways to the supremacy of Christ in his life. Like the 'think parties', these meetings became very popular, with many people commenting that they never heard this sort of thing at church.

So, both within their home and beyond it, Murray and Oda continued faithfully serving their Lord. Evelyn was near them for the remainder of her life, and had moved to live with them shortly before news came of Godfrey's death in 1949. Oda looked after her devotedly as long as she was able, and she died in a nursing home in 1954, her mind sadly clouded. Both Murray and Godfrey had recognized their tremendous debt to her. She had unflaggingly carried out their dying father's request that she should 'live for the boys'. She had provided for them materially a secure home and good education; had inspired and (more difficult) released them to devote their lives to God's service, and with her shrewd common sense had supported them through severe crises. They, on the other hand, had fulfilled more than adequately their obligation to look after her in their father's stead. Not many young men could take their mother with them out to the mission field, and yet manage to escape being psychologically mother-bound, as they both successfully did.

As to the twins, Michael went to Trinity College, Cambridge, and went from strength to strength in his chosen field of medicine. Hanmer too went to Cambridge, but to King's College where he was a member of the famous Chapel choir. Some of his fellow choristers committed their lives to Christ as a result of their friendship with Hanmer, and for a year he was vice-president of the CICCU. He later went successfully into business. Both he and Michael continued, though in a less flamboyant way than their father, to be faithful witnesses for the Lord whom they had early recognized in faraway Dohnavur as the One to command their first respect and love.

In their marriages, both Hanmer and Michael followed the family pattern of choosing partners who were not only dedicated Christians, but also Europeans. Hanmer's wife is Dutch, and Michael's Swiss; thus the links between the Webb-Peploe family and the Continent were reinforced. As Murray observed in his speech at Michael's wedding, 'I am especially happy that in this union my mother's family has, as it were, returned to its homeland. She was a Malan: her great grandfather César Malan, of Geneva, wrote a number of hymns still used in your church today.' No doubt he was equally pleased when Hanmer's marriage to Lucile strengthened the family's Dutch link.

In 1970 an old friend wrote to Murray and Oda to congratulate them on their 'great achievement in the upbringing of your two boys'. The letter is worth quoting as it gives the considered opinion of a respected Christian contemporary of theirs who had watched and pondered the vicissitudes of Murray's career, especially with regard to his family:

> Who would have thought that when the two Webb-Peploe brothers were said to have thrown up all their future to go off to an obscure "orphan home" (our student idea!) in South India in a circumscribed compound and a very feminine set-up—that one day another "M" W-P would reach "imago" stage and discard his chrysalis for St Thomas's chiefdom in cardiology! And who would have thought that when some were saying how misguided M. W-P. was to come home to GP-dom for the sake of the boys' education (and blaming his wife) you'd have such a result! Above all, they are both well on the Lord's side, and look stuck there!

Besides Hanmer and Michael, another young man owed Murray and Oda almost as much, and came to regard Woodley as his home. His name is Peter Pattisson, and his story forms the sequel to the episode of Millicent, the girl with acute appendicitis, recounted in Chapter 9. When Peter was a third-year Cambridge medical student he was invited, although he had only met Murray once before, to stay for a weekend at Woodley. In fact Murray and Oda were coming up to London for the centenary celebrations in 1960 at St

Paul's church, Onslow Square. Murray, as grandson of the
Prebendary, had been asked to speak, and Peter and an
Indian friend had been invited to go back with them for the
weekend. Murray recalled:

> After tea on Sunday I asked Peter what hospital he hoped to go
> on to when he left Cambridge. Rather sadly he replied, "I am not
> sure whether I am going on with medicine or not." It transpired
> that because of his father's unhappiness at his proposal to become
> a medical missionary, he found himself without adequate funds
> to continue. I told him, "I am sure of two things, firstly that God
> does not waste his children's time, and secondly, that he never
> lets down anyone who is trusting him as you are. Let us ask our
> Father about this." So we knelt down and each of us prayed,
> laying the whole matter before our Father in heaven. Later, at
> supper, the telephone rang; it was Millicent, now a married
> woman with two children. She explained that her father would
> soon be coming down to Bournemouth, and was anxious to hand
> over some money to me for the use of some individual in the cause
> of Christ, in gratitude to God for the saving of her life thirty years
> before. I told her briefly of Peter's dilemma, about which I had
> just heard, and Millicent thought that was just the sort of thing
> her father had in mind. The result was that Mr Bulpitt handed
> over to me £500, and Peter was enabled, by dint of earning
> money in his vacation as well, to continue his studies.
>
> Once qualified, he married, and was ready to go abroad, but
> there seemed to be no opening in Korea, the country to which he
> felt that God was calling him. That summer my wife and I were
> invited to attend an international doctors' conference being held
> at Oxford under the auspices of the Christian Medical Fellowship.
> Actually they did not want me at all. They wanted Oda to help to
> entertain the wives of doctors from the Continent. She was
> prevented at the last minute from going but, as we prayed, it
> became clear that I should go none the less. It was at this
> conference that I heard of an urgent need for a doctor to work in
> Korea on a Medical Research Council project on TB of the spine
> in children, and so Peter and his wife went out to Korea and did
> splendid medical work as well as some Scripture Union work in
> nearby churches; later they joined the Overseas Missionary
> Fellowship.

For the rest of Murray's life, Peter regarded Woodley as his
adopted home. He has said that when he stayed there, a

dressing-gowned Murray would wake him at 6 a.m. with a cup of tea. Then silence would reign as each member of the household spent time alone with God. He recognized in this disciplined early rising and in the early nights that made it possible, the well-springs of the sense of the presence of God that many were aware of in that home.

By 1959 Murray's medical practice had grown to such an extent that he needed a partner, and he was joined by Dr Hubert Edmunds who had recently come home from mission work in northern India. Dr Edmunds ran the Barton end of the practice, and Murray the Lymington end. As Dr Edmunds has put it, 'So began a very happy twenty-three years' association with one of the world's outstanding characters. In all the years together I can remember no occasion at all when we had a difference of opinion!' This partnership eased the pressure on Murray, and he and Oda were able more often to accept invitations to act as host and hostess at various student houseparties. A description of this side of Murray's life has been given by Dr Douglas Johnson, who for many years was general secretary first of the Inter Varsity Fellowship and then of the Christian Medical Fellowship:

During his active working life Murray was always popular in the student world. He and Oda were constantly in demand as host and hostess for student house parties and conferences, particularly at St Thomas's and the other London hospitals. His never-ending fund of exquisite humour and the longer anecdotes—often with a pointed moral attached—were a feature at mealtimes. Then, when their very human and fascinatingly interesting host began to talk about his spiritual experience with an unusual passion and seriousness, the effect was startling. In all that really mattered and in all the changing scenes of life, here was someone who was sure of the direction in which he wanted to travel. The words of Scripture took on a new reality when they were so obviously relevant to the doctor's or medical student's daily life. Many a student began a life of Christian discipleship from their meeting with him at one of these house parties or at a hospital Christian Union meeting. Also, from the time of his return to England he set himself to keep the needs of the developing countries of the Third World before his student contacts. He became very successful in this part of his service. For example in

1950 he was invited to address the traditional early morning Annual Breakfast for London medical students, an event initiated in 1891 and continued with only short interruptions during the two world wars until the present day. In 1950 it was again gathering momentum after the Second World War and there were well over one hundred students, with Professor [later, Sir] H. J. Seddon in the chair, to hear Murray present the needs of the Third World, which he did most effectively. It had been arranged that a newly qualified student ("a safe driver") was to pick Murray up from the door and get him to Waterloo to catch the first fast train to Brockenhurst. Murray managed to contain himself until they reached the station, but finding they had fifteen minutes to spare before the train arrived, he lost no time, and the young man was left with no excuse for not seeing how much more needy were the villages of India and the hospitals in the teeming cities there than those in Britain. Having delivered his message, Murray leapt and caught the train. The seed in this case fell on good soil; the young doctor, when he had obtained further necessary qualifications, went out to India, where he proved especially useful as a senior supporter of young Christian medical students.

For several years too, Murray acted as local secretary to the annual conference of the Christian Medical Fellowship that took place in Bournemouth in the second weekend in May. This involved a certain amount of forward planning (arranging hotel bookings and so on), as well as steering the conference through its timetable and organizing excursions in the leisure periods. For all this it was important to have a local man who knew the area well, but equally important was Murray's personality that irradiated the whole conference as he constantly rose to his feet to give out notices, introducing them with some simple but pertinent anecdote which quickly produced a relaxed responsive audience. As he grew older, he loved to assure people that he was in his anecdotage. One of his favourites at Bournemouth was the oft-recounted joke attributed to a Bournemouth councillor, to the effect that 'people come to Bournemouth to die and forget why they have come!'

When Murray felt the time had come to give up this task, he trained his 'curate'—in fact his godson, Dr Christopher Metcalfe, son of his old St Thomas's friend George or 'Paddy'

Metcalfe. When Christopher took over as local secretary to the Christian Medical Fellowship, Murray passed on to him his book of quotable anecdotes. Christopher Metcalfe has given a vivid picture of his godfather as he remembers him shortly after his arrival in England:

> Imagine the excitement of a recently converted Cambridge undergraduate on meeting his long-lost godfather for the first time. This was my privilege at a small Christian Union missionary meeting early in 1948. I remember his theme from 1 Corinthians 1 including the passage, "The foolishness of God is wiser than men"; afterwards the greetings and hand-shake and the walk to my rooms in Jesus College—the long strides and quick characteristic walk in a large pair of brown boots, brown suit, Trinity tie and a hat style that was to become familiar. He was over-joyed to hear my news, responding with his enthusiastic exclamation, "*Won*-derful!" and at the end, "Let's have a pray", was the natural way to close the encounter with simple strong strands drawing things present and future together—and this was always the pattern. I remember too, soon afterwards, my first visit to their lovely Lymington home with its massive and fascinating continental furniture, pictures, portraits, and the wonderful garden; and sitting in the large kitchen with the cats, drinking coffee from Dohnavur-blue cups.

As well as his wider work among students and the medical conferences, Murray continued faithfully with the day-to-day work of the Lymington practice. Dr Edmunds regarded him as 'a very good doctor, one who "knew his stuff". But he was much more than a mere doctor', he added. 'He cared for the whole person, body, soul and spirit. Many a person came seeking healing and found Christ as well.' A few glimpses into his 'doctor's casebook' indicate the quality of care that Murray gave:

> There was the lonely blind old lady, the widow of an MP, and a patient of Murray's. One day he shared with her the good news of Christ's love: 'She was a very peremptory old thing,' he recalled, 'and she asked, "Why has no one ever told me this before?" I said, "Look, when you were in London, did you ever go to church?" "Yes I did, but I switched off—I used to look at the hats." She came to put her trust in Christ and I used to go and read the New Testament to her when I had time.'

Then there was John, a man in his forties who came to the surgery asking for something to help him sleep. Under God's 'traffic control', as Murray saw it, he was the last patient in an evening surgery, so sensing a deeper problem, Murray asked him why he couldn't sleep. It transpired that he had been an officer commanding a double company in the Malayan jungle during the war. His own danger had never worried him, but the hardship and casualties of the men had caused him to break down so that he had spent six months in a psychiatric ward in Singapore. Now he was working as a commercial traveller and expected to drive hundreds of miles in the course of his work. Instead, after 20 or 30 miles he would begin to panic and find himself unable to go on. Murray sensed at once that he was suffering from a deep-rooted fear of death. He gave him something to help him sleep, put him in touch with a London psychiatrist, but also invited him to the next 'think party' and to consider the possibility that Christ could meet his need. Over the next weeks John found Christ's gift of eternal life, and after two or three consultations in London the psychiatrist, also a Christian, wrote that he felt that it was unnecessary to see him again: 'I think he has found the answer.' Soon after this Murray asked John how far he could drive now. 'Oh, several hundred miles and it is going well. I talk to the Lord as I drive,' he said.

Another family were in great distress when they became Murray's patients. The father was an ex-naval man dying of pulmonary tuberculosis, the mother had become an alcoholic, the children were ill-kempt and undernourished. The mother, defiantly insisting at first that 'she could cope', was enabled by Murray's own humility and integrity to admit her need, and turned to Christ, as did the father. Their problems did not vanish forthwith; the father died, but peacefully, and Murray took endless pains with the mother—helping her to get jobs and sticking with her through the difficulties when she lapsed back into alcoholism. This care was typical of him; he took the same sort of trouble when a patient moved to a new area, in trying to find a GP there who would suit. People were amazed at the way in which his care went beyond the ten minutes' consultation in the surgery, to try to meet the needs of the whole man.

This quality of care is seen too in the story of Ann, a nurse who had left a London teaching hospital expecting an illegitimate baby. Working in a nursing home near Lymington until the baby was born, she became Murray's patient. As well as dealing with the necessary antenatal care, he added, 'But you come and have coffee with my wife.' He reported: 'I said to my wife, "There's a girl whom you've never met arriving on your doorstep at 11 tomorrow morning; will you give her some coffee and love her a lot." She is used to this sort of thing, and she agreed.' This was the way in which many deeper needs were met by their splendid partnership. Ann arrived, clearly on the defensive, but after chatting with Oda for some time suddenly the barriers came down and she began to pour out the real troubles, which sprang from her parents having been abroad during her important adolescent years, leaving her with a feeling of being unwanted and without a secure base. Oda was able gently to lead her to Christ, who loves and forgives. A few days later as they were reading Psalm 23 together, they came to the verse 'He restoreth my soul', and Ann said, 'That's just what he is doing for me, isn't it?' They then began to pray about what was to happen to her baby.

When it was born—a son—Ann panicked and got in touch with an adoption society. On the day she was due to sign the papers (God's 'traffic control' again!) she received a letter from an old friend in New Zealand who, knowing about the baby, asked her to come out and marry him. Murray and Oda's final anxieties about her were allayed when an old friend from their Australian days was discovered to be travelling back to Australia on the very boat Ann was booked on, and so they travelled out together with the baby. Apart from its intrinsic interest, this story shows that not only Murray but Oda too had a rare gift for getting alongside people and enabling them to lay bare their real need, then showing them how Christ could meet that need.

In fact, Oda's helping and balancing role was of inestimable value to Murray throughout their married life. As one friend observed:

She is a Christian common sense realist—gold through and through. She was concerned for *depth* of religious experience in Murray's friends and would try to steer off the light-weights and the queer ones. Murray would love them all and be blind to their defects. Oda kept her feet on the ground; she would survey the scene and pronounce what was usually true, when Murray could have been carried away by over-enthusiastic policies or people.

It seems that Oda, with her intelligence, high spirits, determination and common sense, provided just the balance that Murray needed to enable him to serve God most effectively. Possibly, she overestimated her responsibilities: 'I pray,' she told a friend towards the end of Murray's life, 'I shall be able to get him safely tucked up in heaven!'

So the years went by. As well as everything else, Murray was a diocesan lay reader and preached once a month at Hordle Parish Church, some 3 miles from Lymington. Always the pattern of his talks and sermons was the same: Scripture, stories of people past and present or from his own experience, humour, and the direct application to the individual life in the deliberate slow lilting style with pauses that gave people time to absorb.

In 1966 Murray had his seventieth birthday. He and Dr Edmunds retired from the practice, which was taken over by younger men—Dr Ralph Leech, Dr Geoffrey Stanley-Smith and Dr David Mullins. Murray retained a few of his older patients, but gradually they died and his work-load decreased. He continued preaching and addressing groups of students, and the farm and garden took a great deal of his time.

In 1970 he and Oda took on an extra burden that seems to have drained them of almost more energy than even they could spare. An elderly aunt of Murray's, the Great Aunt, or 'G.A.', came to live with them. As Murray wrote, 'She has been ninety for several years—ninety-seven seems to be the actual score. She was living alone, and could no longer cope, and we are sure her being here is right; and what is right means blessing, whether we see it or not.' It was a burden, though, as the old lady needed constant attention. In the process of moving her in, Oda had tripped and fallen downstairs and damaged her wrist, which made matters worse. None the less, Oda was able to lead the 'G.A.' gently into the kingdom of heaven, as Murray reported in a letter to Peter Pattison when the 'G.A.' died:

> She said about two years ago to Mother, 'You know, I am an Archdeacon's daughter and a Canon's widow. I have been to church all my life and taught in Sunday school, but it has all been *outside*, not inside.' Mother explained how by simple faith and the grace of God we can invite the Lord into our hearts and lives— and then he is 'inside'. She said nothing but gradually found peace, lost all her fear of death, and looked forward to meeting him.

Changed though she was, it was not easy looking after the 'G.A.' Oda wrote once, also to Peter Pattison: 'Please don't think we are always saintly about having her. I sometimes feel I could put her out under a bush as some of your African friends do or did!' Eventually it became too much. The 'G.A.' was moved into a nearby nursing home, where Murray and Oda continued to visit her every day until in January 1973 she went to meet her new-found Lord.

Sadly, looking after the aunt seemed to have sapped some vital strength from Oda. It took her some months to regain even some of her vitality, and from now on she became less and less able to cope with people staying in the house. Murray's hearing and eyesight were failing too. One eye became completely useless as a result of a haemmorhage; now the other eye was beginning to go. A letter from Oda to Peter Pattison written in January 1976 described the situation:

> I am glad Françoise told you something about Father. He did not want you to be troubled with it, so neither of us wrote. But now you must know that he is going blind rapidly. The medical verdict is that nothing more can be done for his one remaining eye. He can read only very little, T.V. is still possible. We had a few awful days when first he got the verdict. He was so stunned, had never thought a thing like this would come to him. I was afraid he might not take it from the Lord. But there is peace now and full acceptance, though not without sorrow. He gropes about more and more now, feeling his way. But so dear and cheery and outgoing.

And then Oda added something that, although she probably didn't realize it, was quite as ominous as anything she had written about Murray:

> Abba [their family way of referring to God—Abba, Father] had so wonderfully prepared us for this [Murray's increasing blindness] without our knowing it. About a year ago I was in a very nice meeting in Bournemouth, holding forth, when suddenly I could not find the next word or remember even what the subject had been. I could try switching on to something else and carry on for a while, but then I'd have to stop speaking. Now Father needs somebody all the time. He has a very good 'earing haid'!

This indeed was ominous, as it was the first sign of Oda's progressive loss of memory. However, they carried gamely on. It was in 1976 too that Murray heard of the death of his old friend Howard Somervell: 'He went for a walk with his wife in his beloved hills, near his home at Ambleside, was a little breathless, had a coronary and went Home in a few moments.'

Later that year, Murray had a second eye haemorrhage, but he still could write, using a strong light and a black felt-pen that gave him some ability to read what he had written. Many people still received letters from him in these last years, always written large, bold and black in his characteristic hand. On one he added the comment, 'I hope you can read this; I can't.' He also gave occasional talks, inventing alliterative headings for his topics, and relying on his still excellent memory to lead him through from one topic to the next, as he could no longer read his notes. Oda not only drove him to and from his speaking engagements, but was also at the front with him while he spoke, to read the necessary passages of Scripture.

With his active mind, it was frustrating to be able to do so little. Neighbours or members of the family used to read his letters to him. All through his life he had found his thoughts and feelings expressing themselves readily in verse, and now as he pottered (and tottered—one of his jokes) gently in the garden, he turned to verse more and more. It was easy to remember, and to write it involved comparatively little labour. One such poem was inspired by the tragic news of an accident in Thailand when on 14th January 1978 five missionaries connected with the Overseas Missionary Fellowship hospital at Manorom were killed, together with seven of their children, when returning from a day-long picnic-outing. Several of them had been known to Hanmer and Lucile, using their home in Bangkok for an occasional break. The poem itself appears simple, but pages of Bible references went into its composition:

I make of all my mountains (Is 49:11)

I make of all my mountains
A way to wider lands,
And open for you fountains
In burning desert sands.

I break, like wax, in sunder
The strongest gates of brass,
That all who watch may wonder,
And worship as I pass.

I will unlock the treasure
Of every secret place,
And pour in brimming measure
My all-sufficient grace.

Sure guide, I go before you,
Turn darkness into light;
And lovingly restore you
When wounded in the fight.

I planned the perfect motion
Of sun and moon and stars,
And hold the tides of ocean
Within their bounds and bars.

So is there sea or river
Too wide, too deep to cross?
Or can I not deliver
From fear and foe and loss?

I will give praise for sadness,
For sorrow songs of joy,
My everlasting gladness
Which nothing can destroy.

Go, live and love and labour
For others night and day,
Count everyone your neighbour
And shew to each my way.

Then this shall be the token
That you are sent by me:
The bound, the blind, the broken
Are loved, and healed and free.

Murray had two major operations for arthritis towards the end of his life, both largely successful; a hip-replacement in 1978 and a knee-joint replacement in 1979. A delay in leaving St Thomas's hospital after one of these led to the characteristic comment: 'Disappointments are His appointments, so all is well.'

Gradually the animals had to go, the goats first, the pigs and then the geese. The hens stayed for a time until Oda could no longer cope with them. Hubert Edmunds recalled: 'I called in one morning and found Murray trying to mend the hen-house, as they were often visited by foxes. The nearest I ever heard to a complaint from him was his joking observation: "It's difficult trying to knock a nail when you can't see where to hit!"'

Murray always managed to laugh at his and Oda's disabilities. Here are some of his vivid descriptions, funny as well as sad, of their last years:

August 1979: 'Mother is fit but gets tired and her memory and words often fail. I'm half deaf, half blind, half lame and more than half senile, but as long as we can muster one sound organ and limb between us we can totter and potter on adequately till the Angels' Sky train calls ['Better than Freddie Laker's', he comments elsewhere!]—and it reinforces that "end of term feeling". We are going Home for the holidays soon, and then what WON'T we do!'

October 1980: 'I can't hear what Mother says, and if I ask her to say it again she has forgotten what she said!'

In fact Oda's memory was worsening rapidly. The cause was cerebral atrophy and nothing could be done. Soon she had to give up driving, a sad loss to them both. They wondered seriously whether they should leave Woodley, but decided not to as there at least Murray could find his way about. Michael, busy though he was, came down nearly every Saturday to help; someone was providentially found who would cook and look after things a bit, and their old helpers rallied round. And so for Murray the final 'end of term' drew near.

Hubert Edmunds has described what happened:

> My last contact with Murray was a few minutes before he died. I had called with some apples. Mrs Rapley, their wonderful helper, said, 'Oh, Dr Webb-Peploe isn't very well. He's in bed', so I went up to see him. He seemed to think he had flu, and asked what he owed for the apples. When I had taken the money, I decided that if he had flu he probably would not feel like chatting so I said goodbye, little knowing that it was for the last time. As I went out through the pantry they were getting coffee ready, and while he was drinking his some ten minutes later, he collapsed with a heart attack. The mercy was that it happened in the morning when Mrs Rapley was there. Dr Mullins was called and took him to Lymington hospital. He felt that for Oda's sake every effort to resuscitate him should be made, but nothing could be done.

Murray had gone straight into the presence of his Lord, and nothing could bring him back. And yet he had lived in that presence every day. He loved in his latter years to think that the believer would hardly notice death (Jn 8:51 AV—'If a man shall keep my saying, he shall never see death'),[1] it would be just like walking from one room in the Father's house to another, in deep conversation with a much loved Friend. And so it was for him.

'How will *you* go?' he would sometimes ask. 'Gladly?'

Notes

Foreword

1. From Amy Carmichael *Gold Cord*, (SPCK, 1932), p.302, used by permission of the Christian Literature Crusade, Fort Washington, and SPCK, London.

Chapter 1

1. H. W. Webb-Peploe, '*The Life of Privilege, Possession, Peace and Power*', addresses delivered at the Northfield Convention, Massachussetts, August 1895, p.67.

Chapter 2

1. Rudyard Kipling, *Mulholland's Contract*, reprinted by permission of the National Trust.

Chapter 3

1. Quoted in Liddell Hart's *History of the First World War* (Pan Books, 1972), ch.6, p.243.
2. It is now in the First World War Archive at Sunderland Polytechnic, together with Murray's wartime letters.
3. *Daily Light* is a selection of morning and evening readings from Scripture, originally selected by Samuel Bagster. For over a century it has given daily light and guidance to many thousands of Christians.

Chapter 4

1. Leonard Woolf, *Downhill All the Way* (Hogarth Press, 1975), p.1.

2. Vera Brittain, *Testament of Youth* (Victor Gollancz, 1933), p.469.

3. Basil Willey, in *Promise of Greatness—The 1914–18 War*, ed. George A. Panichas (Cassell, 1968).

4. V. H. H. Green, *Religion at Oxford and Cambridge* (SCM, 1964), p.332.

5. Cartoon in *The Pip*, cadets' commemorative publication.

6. Brittain, *Testament of Youth*, p.497.

7. Malcolm Muggeridge, *Chronicles of Wasted Time*, vol. I: *The Green Stick* (Collins, 1972), p.78.

8. Evangelical: 'That section of the Christian community that emphasizes the reliability and final authority of the Bible and whose message focuses on the finished work of Christ for our forgiveness' (Oliver Barclay, *Whatever Happened to the Jesus Lane Lot?* (IVP, 1977), p.154, note 2).

9. Godfrey Buxton is descended from Sir Thomas Fowell Buxton (1786–1845), who worked for the abolition of slavery and who married Hannah Gurney, sister of Elizabeth Fry.

10. For details of the Mission, which from the CICCU point of view was not a complete success, see J. C. Pollock, *A Cambridge Movement* (John Murray, 1953), pp.199–200.

11. From *Basil's Recollections* (copy at Tyndale House, Cambridge).

Chapter 5

1. Frances Donaldson, *Edward VIII* (Omega, 1976), p.83.

2. Oliver Barclay, *Whatever Happened to the Jesus Lane Lot?* (IVP, 1977), pp.98–99.

3. Archibald Glover, *A Thousand Miles of Miracle in China* (Pickering & Inglis, 1904).

Chapter 6

1. R. T. Archibald, 'My Last Eight Months in India' (CSSM, 1925).

2. From the Prayer Letter of the Cambridge University Missionary Band, autumn 1925.

Chapter 7

1. 'In these days he went out to the mountain to pray; and

all night he continued in prayer to God' (Lk 6:12, RSV).

2. This wording is not quite the same as in any of our versions; according to Murray it is based on the French. At any rate, the key verbs are the same as in the AV.

3. E. B. Pusey, *The Minor Prophets, with a Commentary* (Nisbet, 1907): 'And to the hushed soul, hushed to itself and its own thoughts, hushed in awe of his majesty and his presence, before his face, God speaks.'

4. The Dohnavur Fellowship became independent from CEZMS in 1925.

5. Amy Carmichael, *Gold Cord* (SPCK, 1932), p.208.

6. From *Dohnavur Letter*, no. 7 (January 1926).

7. Ibid.

8. Ibid.

9. It was at Joppa on the coast of Israel that Peter received the vision already mentioned in this chapter.

10. Godfrey noted that the Bible passages through which God spoke to him on October 28th were these: Mt 18:14 ('So it is not the will of my Father who is in heaven that one of these little ones should perish', RSV) came when he first left England, and with it Mt 14:27–29 (AV):

    'It is I; be not afraid' ...

    'Lord, if it be thou, bid me come unto thee on the water' ...

    'Come.'

    And when Peter was come down out of the ship, he walked on the water, to go to Jesus.

11. 'Then went king David in, and sat before the Lord, and he said, Who am I, O Lord God? and what is my house, that thou has brought me hitherto? And this was yet a small thing in thy sight, O Lord God; but thou hast spoken also of thy servant's house for a great while to come' (AV).

12. Carmichael, *Gold Cord*, p.279.

Chapter 8

1. *Dohnavur Letter*, no. 13 (March 1928).

2. *Dohnavur Letter*, no. 16 (February 1929).

3. *Dohnavur Letter*, no. 16 (February 1929).

4. *Dohanvur Letter*, no. 17 (May 1929).

5. Amy Carmichael, *Gold Cord* (SPCK, 1932), p.287.
6. Ibid., p.289.
7. *Dohnavur Letter*, no. 17 (May 1929).
8. It is interesting to note that Howard Somervell records removing an ovarian cyst weighing 112 pounds at Neyyoor (*After Everest* [Hodder & Stoughton, 1936], p.309).
9. *Annachie* means literally 'elder brother'. It was the name given to all men workers at Dohnavur, both Indian and foreign.
10. Bishop Houghton, *Amy Carmichael of Dohnavur* (SPCK, 1953), pp. 282 and 355–56).

Chapter 9

1. Bishop Houghton, *Amy Carmichael of Dohnavur* (SPCK, 1953) p.263.

Chapter 10

1. Epaphroditus: a messenger between Paul and the church at Philippi. See Phil 2:25–30 and Phil 4:18.
2. From the first issue of a new newsletter, *Dust of Gold* (February–June 1933).
3. Amy Carmichael, *Windows* (SPCK, 1937), p.14.
4. Amy Carmichael, *Though the Mountains Shake* (Madras, 1943), p.46.
5. Caleb Josh 14:6–14
6. Carmichael, *Windows*, ch. 31.

Chapter 11

1. Amy Carmichael, *Windows* (SPCK, 1937), p.105.
2. Nancy E. Robbins, *Greater Is He* (SPCK, 1952), p.37.
3. Carmichael, *Windows*, op. cit., p.137.
4. Ibid., p.193.
5. Nancy E. Robbins, *Not Forgetting to Sing* (Hodder & Stoughton, 1967), p.32; also Robbins, *Greater Is He*, p.31.
6. *Dust of Gold* (May 1939).

Chapter 12

1. T. Howard Somervell, *After Everest* (Hodder & Stoughton, 1936), p.155.

2. James Morris, *Heaven's Command* (Penguin Books, 1979), p.72.
3. Bishop Houghton, *Amy Carmichael of Dohnavur* (SPCK, 1953), p.362.
4. C. G. Webb-Peploe, 'Field Notes on the Mammals of South Tinnevelly, South India, *Journal of the Bombay Natural History Society* (April 1947).

Chapter 13

1. Murray had in mind here the comment made by Archbishop William Temple on this verse: 'The Lord does not promise that anyone who keeps his word shall avoid the physical incident called death; but that if his mind is turned towards that word it will not pay any attention to death; death will be to it irrelevant. It happens to him, but he does not in any full sense see it or notice it' (*Readings in John's Gospel*, Macmillan, 1955), p.147.